THE

TESTIMONY OF GOD

AGAINST SLAVERY,

OR A

COLLECTION OF PASSAGES FROM THE BIBLE,

WHICH SHOW THE

SIN OF HOLDING PROPERTY IN MAN.

With Notes.

BY REV. LA ROY SUNDERLAND.

> How canst thou say, I am not polluted? See thy way in the valley; know what thou hast done.— *In thy skirts is found the* BLOOD OF THE SOULS OF THE POOR INNOCENTS. — Yet thou sayest, Because I am *innocent,* surely his anger shall turn from me; behold, I will plead with thee, because thou sayest, I have not *sinned.* JER. 2: 23—35.

BOSTON:
PUBLISHED BY WEBSTER & SOUTHARD,
No. 9, Cornhill.
1835.

Republished, 1970
Scholarly Press, 22929 Industrial Drive East
St. Clair Shores, Michigan 48080

Library of Congress Catalog Card Number: 73-92444
Standard Book Number 403-00183-8

Entered according to Act of Congress, in the year 1835, by
LA ROY SUNDERLAND,
in the Clerk's office of the District Court of Massachusetts.

This edition is printed on a high-quality,
acid-free paper that meets specification
requirements for fine book paper referred
to as "300-year" paper

WEBSTER & SOUTHARD,

NO. 9, CORNHILL, BOSTON,

HAVE IN PRESS, AN

ANTI-SLAVERY ALMANAC,

For the year **1836,** to be issued before the first day of September, 1835. It will consist of original matter by the most popular anti-slavery writers, together with selections from the numerous works on slavery now before the public. It will contain,

1. The customary astronomical calculations, for the meridians of Boston, New York and Pittsburgh, and important and useful information of a general character.
2. Accurate statistical information, as far as can be ascertained, respecting the past history and present state of slavery in the United States, together with a brief view of the system as upheld by law.
3. A condensed view of the principles on which Anti-Slavery Societies are founded.
4. Accurate statistical information respecting the formation, progress and present condition of Anti-Slavery Societies in this country.
5. A list of all the important books and periodicals on the subject of slavery.
6. Poetry, anecdotes, &c. applicable to the subject, original and select.
7. Short addresses to Members of Congress, Ministers, Christians, females, the inhabitants of the free states generally, the free people of color, and slave-holders.
8 Facts and arguments showing the safety of immediate emancipation.
9. The superiority of free labor over slave labor, as it respects economy and productiveness.

It is intended that all the articles shall be short, pithy, and comprehensive, and we shall use our utmost exertions to make it a powerful auxiliary to the cause of emancipation. We feel confident that all the friends of the cause of universal liberty will use their influence to extend its circulation as widely as possible. It will contain 48 pages duodecimo, on handsome brevier type, and will be printed on good paper, and ornamented with engravings.

We have engaged the assistance of J. G. Birney, Charles Stuart, A. A. Phelps, S. J. May, H. B. Stanton, Mrs. Child, and many other popular writers, and can therefore promise that all the articles it contains will be of a high character.

We are very anxious to give a correct list of all the Anti-Slavery Societies in the United States, in the form given below. There are many Societies, in and out of New England, from which our information is very incomplete. From most of the Societies of Vermont we have no report, except the name of the Society. We would respectfully request all the Secretaries of Anti-Slavery Societies to report immediately (post paid) to Webster & Southard, 9, Cornhill, Boston. Communications appropriate to the Almanac will be gratefully received.

It is very important, for the success of the cause of emancipation, that Anti-Slavery Societies should act in harmony, and co-operate with one another. A correct list of the Societies will greatly facilitate such co-operation, and subserve many other useful purposes. We hope that all secretaries of Societies will be prompt in forwarding information.

Boston June 3d, 1835.

Name.	Date.	No.	Pres.	Secretary.
Dorchester, Mass	May 1835	186	Samuel Mullikin	Rev. David Sanford
Providence R. I.	June 1833	101	Josiah Cady	Benj. L. Farnsworth
" Juvenile	Dec 1835	35	Sarah Miller	Almira Bolles
" Ladies	1834	101	Mrs. Lucy Blain	Miss Hannah Farnum

Note. The second column shows the time when the Soc. was formed;—the 3d the number of members;—the 4th and 5th the names of the President and Corresponding Secretary, if there is one; if not, the name of the Recording do.

W. & S. have on hand a few copies of the second edition of the **REVIEW** of the **LADY SUPERIOR'S REPLY** to "SIX MONTHS IN A CONVENT," being a Vindication of Miss Reed. Price 20 cents.

A DISQUISITION ON THE EVILS OF USING TOBACCO,

and the necessity of IMMEDIATE and entire reformation. Just published by WM. PEIRCE, at 9, Cornhill.

This little pamphlet, of 24 pages, written by Rev. Mr. Fowler of Fall River, is worthy of a perusal by every inhabitant of the United States. Benevolent individuals may confer a lasting benefit on their respective neighborhoods, by circulating this work.

CONTENTS.

PRELIMINARY REMARKS, - - - - - - 9

CHAPTER I.— Extracts from the writings of MOSES, - 12

CHAPTER II.— Extracts from the writings of MOSES, - 17

CHAPTER III.— Extracts from the writings of JOSHUA, JOB, and EZRA, - - - - - - - - - 29

CHAPTER IV.— Extracts from the writings of DAVID, 37

CHAPTER V.— Extracts from the writings of SOLOMON, 43

CHAPTER VI.— Extracts from the writings of ISAIAH, 50

CHAPTER VII.— Extracts from the writings of JEREMIAH, 58

CHAPTER VIII.— Extracts from the writings of EZEKIEL, DANIEL, HOSEA, JOEL, AMOS, MICAH, NAHUM, HABBAKKUK, ZECHARIAH AND MALACHI, - - - - - 65

CHAPTER IX.— Extracts from the writings of ST. MATTHEW, ST. MARK, ST. LUKE, AND ST. JOHN, containing many of the sayings and PRECEPTS of JESUS CHRIST, - - 70

CHAPTER X.— Extracts from the Epistles of ST. PAUL, 80

CHAPTER XI.— Extracts from the Epistles of ST. JAMES, ST. PETER, AND ST. JOHN. - - - - - - 93

PREFACE.

If Slavery is ever abolished from the world, it will be done by the influence of the Christian Religion. Men never will abandon slave-holding, till they feel it to be a sin against God; and the reason why all who are now concerned in the support of this system, do not feel and act under this conviction is, because they have not examined it in the light of God's word.

It is a solemn fact, that there is scarcely any one *sin* described in the inspired writings, in all its parts, features and consequences, so clearly and explicitly, as is *the sin of holding property in man;* and scarcely any other sin has been so frequently denounced in the Bible, with the fearful maledictions of Heaven. Let the reader examine the few passages quoted in the following pages, with a prayerful and unprejudiced mind, and let him ask himself, while doing this, what we may suppose God's design was, in dictating so much which we find in the Scriptures against *oppression* in all its forms, against *man-stealing*, against *defrauding the poor* of his right, and against *keeping back the hire* which is due to those who reap down our fields? Why has he, in so many instances, enjoined it upon man to show pity towards those of his species who are in distress, and to extend relief to all who are in trouble and unable to help themselves? Such passages, it will be perceived, make up no inconsiderable portion of the preceptive part of the Bible, and must these all be thrown away? Is there no sin committed by any of the human family now, against, which they were designed to bear? Are not these passages of Holy Scripture, now "*profitable for doctrine, for reproof, for correction, and for instruction in righteousness?*"

In a word, who does not see, that if no part of the Scriptures may now be brought to bear, with the utmost propriety, against the present *system of oppression* which prevails in this nation, merely because the circumstances under which this sin is now committed may differ, in some respects, from those in which men sinned when the various parts of the Bible were at first written, then it must follow, as an undeniable consequence, that no sins of any kind, can be reproved, at the present day, in Scripture language, nor from Scripture authority.

It is not pretended that all the passages in the Bible, which relate to this subject, are brought forward in this little work, but it has been the author's design to notice the most of those which, it is believed, either directly or indirectly, show *slave-holding* to be a *sin;* and to do justice to the subject, none of those are omitted which have been so frequently quoted, and so strangely *tortured* to prove that the Bible justifies the system.

The work is divided into chapters, and the different authors or writers, from which the passages are quoted, are named at the head of each chapter. The notes are numbered to correspond with the texts upon which they are written.

This work has been prepared with the kindest of feelings, both toward the *enslaver* and the *enslaved*, and if it should be the means of helping the friends of these two classes of our fellow-citizens, in any degree, to the use of those *heavenly weapons*, by which it is our duty to prosecute the great and good work of delivering the *oppressed* from the hands of the *oppressor*, the object will have been obtained. *For the weapons of our warfare are not carnal, but mighty through God, to the pulling down of strong holds; casting down imaginations, and every high thing that exalteth itself against the knowledge of God.*

June 3, 1835.

TESTIMONY OF GOD

AGAINST SLAVERY.

PRELIMINARY REMARKS.

What is slavery? Especially, what is that kind of slavery which prevails in this country, and against which, it is believed, the testimony of God is directed in the passages of Scripture quoted in the following pages? It is very necessary to settle this inquiry, before we proceed to examine what the inspired writers have said; inasmuch as without a satisfactory answer to this question, it will be impossible to tell whether any portion of God's word may be brought to bear against it, consistently with the design of the Holy Spirit in the gift of the inspired writings.

1. We observe, then, that by *slavery*, in this country, is meant, *the possession and holding of the human species as property;—the using them not as human beings, but as things and beasts, exacting of them services and compelling them to perform labors without rendering them any just equivalent in return, and without an equal view to their own benefit.* This kind of slavery may be distinguished by the following remarkable particulars.

2. It gives the master an arbitrary power over the peace, the health and life of the slave. That is, the master may compel the slave to endure hardships, and to perform labors which are inhumanly wasting to his health and life.

3. It violently deprives the slave of his *right to himself*, his right to the free use of his own will, reason, judgment, and labors.

4. It deprives him of all adequate protection for his person, his character and morals.

5. It crushes and kills the human mind, by violently withholding and preventing all suitable instruction in letters and science.

6. It shortens human life, by violently compelling the slave to endure rigorous hardships, and to perform excessive labors.

7. Its direct and legitimate tendency and influence on the minds of both the enslaver and the enslaved is, to deaden the conscience, and prevent the salvation of the soul.

8. On the part of the enslaved, it is *involuntary*. They are violently made slaves, at their birth or afterwards. No one who is now a slave in this land, in the above sense, has entered into this state voluntarily, of his own accord. Those who are slaves have been violently made such, and they are now kept in this state by force and arms.

9. It is perpetual in its duration, descending from one generation to another; — it is a power over the peace, purity, health, character, liberty, (life and salvation) of the slave, which nothing but the will or consent of the master can dissolve.*

10. Such are a few of the features by which this system may be distinguished from anything and everything which was ever tolerated by the God of the Bible, under the name of servitude or slavery. It is true that a certain kind of slavery was tolerated by some of the Old Testament writers; but then it differed radically from the system of slave-holding, which prevails now in these United States; and besides, if any kind of slavery may be tolerated now, under the gospel dispensation, because a certain species of it existed among the Jews anciently, or because Christ and his Apostles did not say in just so many words, that " slave-holding under all circumstances of the case, is a sin against God," then it follows by the same rules of interpretation; —

11. That polygamy is justifiable now, by the Bible, for some of the patriarchs were polygamists, and they carried out their views by their practice. Abraham had two wives, David had two, and so of

---

* For the authority upon which the above statements are made, and for any others of the same kind which may be found in the following pages, I would here, once for all, refer the reader to Stroud's Law of Slavery, Rankin's Letters on Slavery, Torry's Portraiture of Slavery ; and the laws of the States generally, where slavery is legalized.

others that might be mentioned; Solomon had seven hundred wives, and three hundred concubines; and where is it said in the Bible that "polygamy is a sin?"

12. Private revenge and murder may be justified, at the present time in the very same way. It was a practice which prevailed among the patriarchs, and it was tolerated by the law of Moses in precisely the same way that the Mosaic law allowed of slavery. Hence the nearest relation had a right to kill the murderer of his friend, without trial, judge or jury. See Numb. 35: 19.

13. Many other practices, were tolerated and legalized by the Jewish law, such as offensive wars, and wars for the utter extermination of whole nations of idolaters. By this law it was made the duty of a man to marry his brother's widow, and the duty of masters, in certain cases, to marry his female slave, or to set her free.

14. Again, if the silence of Christ may be referred to as a justification of slavery, then, by this same silence, we may justify the making selling and drinking of ardent spirits; if Christ never condemned slavery, then neither did he condemn masonry, nor anti-masonry, nor polygamy, nor lotteries, nor theatres, nor offensive wars, nor tyranny of any kind, nor gladiatorial exhibitions, a kind of game which was much in fashion when he was upon earth, and which formed some of the most horrid and bloody scenes upon which the eyes of man ever gazed. If Christ never condemned slavery, by calling it by name, and denouncing it expressly, as a *sin*, then neither did he condemn the doctrine of purgatory, of transubstantiation, of indulgencies, and numerous other pernicious errors, which even in his day, had a "local habitation and a name."

15. If the Apostles may be referred to, as justifying any system of slavery, when they direct servants to be obedient to their masters; then it follows, that they sanctioned the tyranny and bloody cruelties of Nero, when they commanded Christians to be obedient to Magistrates; and by the same rule also, Christ justified persecution, when he commanded his disciples to pray for those who persecuted them. But the Apostles did as really condemn the relation which existed between the master and the slave, whom he held as his entire property, as they did condemn the injustice, the cruelty, and the murder which that relation allowed; for the Apostles could not have condemned the things which that relation gave the slave holder a right to do, and at the same time not condemn the relation which authorized him to do them.

CHAPTER I.

MOSES.

The bondage of the Israelites in Egypt, and the measures which God took to liberate them.

1. And the LORD said, I have surely seen the affliction of my people which are in Egypt, and have heard their cry by reason of their task-masters; for I know their sorrows. Ex. 3: 7.

Now therefore, behold, the cry of the children of Israel is come unto me; and I have also seen the oppression wherewith the Egyptians oppress them. Ex. 3: 9.

3. And it came to pass, in process of time, that the king of Egypt died; and the children of Israel sighed by reason of the bondage, and they cried, and their cry came up unto God, by reason of the bondage. And God heard their groaning, and God remembered his covenant, and God looked upon the children of Israel, and God had respect unto them. Ex. 2: 23.

4. Thus saith the LORD God of the Hebrews, let my people go, that they may serve me. Ex. 9: 1.

5. Thus saith the LORD God of the Hebrews, How long wilt thou refuse to humble thyself before me? let my people go that they may serve me. Ex. 10: 3.

6. And Pharaoh commanded the same day, the task-masters of the people, and their officers saying,

Ye shall no more give the people straw to make brick, as heretofore; let them go and gather straw for themselves. And the tale of the bricks, which they did make heretofore, ye shall lay upon them; ye shall not diminish aught thereof; for they be idle; therefore they cry, saying, Let us go and sacrifice to our God. Ex. 5: 6.

7. So the people were scattered abroad throughout all the land of Egypt to get their stubble instead of straw. And the task-masters hasted them saying, Fulfil your works, your daily tasks, as when there was straw. Ex. 5: 12.

8. And the officers of the children of Israel, which Pharaoh's task-masters had set over them, were beaten, and demanded, Wherefore have ye not fulfilled your task in making brick, both yesterday and to day, as heretofore? Ex. 5: 14.

9. And the officers of the children of Israel did see that they were in evil case, after it was said, Ye shall not diminish aught from your bricks of your daily task. And they met Moses and Aaron, who stood in the way, as they came forth from Pharaoh; and they said unto them, The LORD look upon you, and judge; because ye have made our savour to be abhorred in the eyes of Pharaoh, and in the eyes of his servants to put a sword in their hand to slay us. Ex. 5: 19.

10. And Moses returned unto the LORD, and said, LORD wherefore hast thou so evil entreated this people? Why is it that thou hast sent me? For since I come to Pharaoh to speak in thy name, he hath done evil to this people, neither hast thou delivered thy people at all. Ex. 5: 22.

11. And God spake unto Moses, and said unto him, I am the LORD; I have also heard the groan-

ing of the children of Israel, whom the Egyptians keep in bondage; and I have remembered my covenant. Wherefore say unto the children of Israel, I am the LORD, and I will bring you out from under the burdens of the Egyptians, and I will rid you out of their bondage. Ex. 6: 2.

12. And Moses spake so unto the children of Israel, but they hearkened not unto Moses for anguish, of spirit and for cruel bondage. Ex. 6: 9.

NOTES ON CHAPTER I.

1. *I have surely seen the afflictions of my people.*

The people of God, at this time were held in slavery by the Egyptians; and though the bondage which they were compelled to endure, was certainly not so cruel and severe as that which nearly three millions of American citizens are now doomed to suffer; yet the Infinite Being manifested the most feeling pity for their sorrows. And how can a believer in the truth of the Bible suppose, for one moment, that this same unchangeable God is now an indifferent spectator merely, to the accumulated wrongs which thousands of the poor slaves are forced to endure in this Christian land, — thousands who are his people, who love him, but who are not permitted to read his word, nor to worship him according to the dictates of their own consciences?

2. *I have also seen their oppression.*

Oppression is the spoiling or taking an other's goods or the fruit of his own labor by constraint, terror or force; and men commit this crime whenever they offer any violence to the persons, or estates, or consciences of others. If the Israelites were oppressed by the Egyptians, what may be said of millions of the human species in this land, who are every day robbed of the fruit of their own labor?

3. *And God heard their groanings.*

And does he not not now hear the groanings of the enslaved? Has he no respect unto the sighings of millions who now cry unto him by reason of their chains?

4. *Let my people go.*

And now, if God uttered his testimony against the slavery which his people endured thousands of years ago, and if he commanded their oppressors to let them go free, how can it be made to appear, that he does not do this now?

5. *And Pharaoh commanded the task-masters.*

The persons who were placed over the slaves in Egypt, were denominated "task-masters," it was their office to appoint them their work, and exact its daily performance. In the Hebrew they are called, "princes of burdens," and in the Septuagint, "overseers of the works;" in the dialect of this land, these officers are called "overseers," "masters," and "soul-drivers."

6. *Ye shall not diminish aught thereof.*

And how often Pharaoh has been denounced as a most unmerciful tyrant, for his having made this oppressive requisition! And this too, by thousands who seem never to have thought, that similar exactions have been imposed upon the slaves of this land. Their "masters," tell us the slaves must not, and cannot, and shall not be set free, till they are fit, or prepared to make a good use of their freedom; and yet these very "masters," are constantly devising means to strengthen the chains by which the slaves have been and still are, degraded and made incapable (as they say) of taking care of themselves. Though these same slaves now support themselves and their "masters," besides, with their chains on, yet we are told, that if their chains were to be taken off, they could not and would not even take care of themselves!

That the people of the South are really desirous of preparing their slaves to enjoy their liberty, if indeed, they should ever be favored with it, take the following in evidence; it is an act lately passed by the State of South Carolina, "To *amend* the laws in relation to the slaves and free persons of color."

"Sec. 2. Be it enacted by the Honorable, the Senate and House of Representatives, now met and sitting in General Assembly, and by the authority of the same; if any person shall hereafter teach any slave to read or write, or shall aid or assist in teaching slaves to read or write, or cause or procure any slave to read or write; such person, if a free white person, upon conviction thereof, shall for each and every offence against this act, be fined, not exceeding one hundred dollars, and imprisoned not more than six months, or if a free person of color, shall be whipped not exceeding fifty lashes, and fined not exceeding fifty dollars, at the discretion of the Court of Magistrates and free holders before whom such free person of color is tried, and if a slave, shall be whipped at the discretion of the court, not exceeding fifty lashes; the informer to be entitled to one half of the fine, and to be a competent witness; and if any free person of color or slave shall keep any school or other place of instruction for teaching any slave or free person of color to read or write, such free person of color or slave, shall be liable to the same fine, imprisonment or corporeal punishment, as are by this section imposed and inflicted on free persons of color or slaves, for teaching slaves to read or write."

"SEC. 2. If any person shall employ or keep as a clerk, any slave or free person of color, or shall permit any slave or free person of color, to act as a clerk or salesman, in or about any shop, store or house, used for trading, such person shall be liable to be indicted therefor, and upon conviction thereof, shall be fined for each and every offence, not exceeding one hundred dollars, and be imprisoned not exceeding six months; the informer to be a competent witness, and to be entitled to one half of the fine."

7. *They were in an evil case.*

Sure enough they were. The slaves of this age, cannot be set free, because, forsooth, they are not properly instructed, and the above and many other similar laws declare, under the penalties of *whipping, fine, imprisonment* and DEATH, that the slaves must not, and shall not be instructed, lest they should be set free, or by this means obtain their liberty ! This is certainly an "*evil* case."

8. *Ye have made our savour to be abhorred in the eyes of Pharaoh.*

So it seems those Israelites did really find their bondage increased by the very efforts which God and his servants were making to get them free. But Moses did not consider this a sufficient reason why he should cease to plead for their freedom. And shall we, of the present age, forbear to preach the truth because some sinners will not repent ? Does it alter the course of our duty, when some "harden their hearts," and "wax worse and worse," after they "have received the holy commandment delivered unto them ?" If not, why then should we be so often reproached with having retarded the abolition of slavery in this land ? And this is the strongest, and in fact, about the only objection which many serious and good people can bring against the Anti-Slavery movements of of the present day. We try to do something, — *they* do nothing, except to denounce our means and measures, yet we "retard the abolition of slavery!" The Lord be judge, between us and them.

There can be no doubt but that the hearts of many "masters," in this nation, are now hardened in precisely the same way, that Pharaoh's was, and God has just as much agency in hardening their hearts now, as he ever had in hardening the heart of Pharaoh. God says now, as he has long been doing to them, "Let these slaves go free!" and they hear this voice of God in the dictates of reason and humanity, they hear it in the precepts of the Bible, and they acknowledge it in the great charter of our national existence; yet they refuse to obey it, and in doing so, they harden their hearts.

CHAPTER II.

MOSES.

The different kinds of servitude allowed among the Hebrews.

1. If thou buy an Hebrew servant, six years he shall serve; and in the seventh he shall go out free for nothing. Ex. 21: 2.

2. And if a man sell his daughter to be a maid-servant, she shall not go out as the men-servants do. If she please not her master who hath betrothed her unto himself, then shall he let her be redeemed, to sell her unto a strange nation he shall

have no power, seeing he hath dealt deceitfully with her. And if he have betrothed her unto his son, he shall deal with her after the manner of daughters. If he take him another wife; her food, her raiment, and her duty of marriage, shall he not diminish. And if he do not these three unto her, then shall she go out free without money. Ex. 21: 7.

3. If a thief be found breaking up — he should make full restitution; if he have nothing, then he shall be sold for his theft. Ex. 22: 2.

4. And if a man smite his servant or his maid, with a rod, and he die under his hand; he shall be surely punished. Notwithstanding, if he continue a day or two, he shall not be punished, for he is his money. Ex. 21: 20.

5. And he that stealeth a man and selleth him, or if he be found in his hand, he shall surely be put to death. Ex. 21: 16.

6. Thou shalt neither vex a stranger, nor oppress him; for ye were strangers in the land of Egypt. Ye shall not afflict any widow or fatherless child. If thou afflict them in any wise, and they cry at all unto me, I will surely hear their cry, and my wrath shall wax hot, and I will kill you with the sword; and your wives shall be widows and your children fatherless. Ex. 22: 21.

7. Ye shall not steal neither deal falsely, neither lie one to another. Lev. 19: 11.

8. Thou shalt not defraud thy neighbor, neither rob him; the wages of him that is hired shall not abide with thee all night until the morning. Lev. 19: 13.

9. Thou shalt not curse the deaf, nor put a stumbling block before the blind, but shalt fear thy God. Lev. 19: 14.

10. Thou shalt not avenge nor bear any grudge against the children of thy people, but thou shalt love thy neighbor as thyself; I am the Lord. Lev. 19 : 18.

11. And if thy brother be waxen poor, and fallen in decay with thee, then thou shalt relieve him ; yea, though he be a stranger, or a sojourner ; that he may live with thee. Lev. 25 : 35.

12. And if thy brother that dwelleth by thee be waxen poor, and be sold unto thee, thou shalt not compel him to serve as a bond-servant. But as an hired servant, and as a sojourner, he shall be with thee, and shall serve thee unto the year of jubilee; and then shall he depart from thee, — for they are my servants — they shall not be sold as bond-men. Thou shalt not rule over him with rigor but shalt fear thy God. Lev. 25 : 39.

13. Both thy bond-men, and thy bond-maids which thou shalt have, shall be of the heathen that are round about you ; of them shall ye buy bond-men and bond-maids. Lev. 25 ; 44.

14. And if ye go to war in your land against the enemy that oppresseth you, then ye shall blow an alarm with the trumpets; and ye shall be remembered before the Lord your God, and ye shall be saved from your enemies. Num. 10 : 9.

15. Thou shalt not steal, neither shalt thou desire thy neighbor's wife, neither shalt thou covet thy neighbor's house, his field, or his man-servant, or his maid-servant, his ox, or his ass, or anything that is thy neighbors. Deut. 5 : 19, 21.

16. For the Lord your God is God of gods, and Lord of lords, a great God, a mighty, and a terrible, which regardeth not persons, nor taketh reward. He doth execute the judgment of the fath-

erless and widow, and loveth the stranger, in giving him food and raiment; love Ye, therefore, the stranger; for ye were strangers in the land of Egypt. Deut. 10: 17.

17. If there be among you a poor man of one of thy brethren within any of thy gates, in thy land which the LORD thy God giveth thee, thou shalt not harden thine heart, nor shut thine hand from thy poor brother; but thou shalt open thine hand wide unto him, and shalt surely lend him sufficient for his need, in that which he wanteth. Deut. 15: 7.

18. Beware that there be not a thought in thy wicked heart, saying, The seventh year the year of release, is at hand; and thine eye be evil against thy poor brother, and thou givest him nought; and he cry unto the LORD against thee, and it be sin unto thee. Deut. 15: 9.

19. Thou shalt surely give him, and thine heart shall not be grieved when thou givest unto him; because that for this thing the LORD thy God shall bless thee in all thy works, and in all that thou puttest thine hand unto. Deut. 15: 10.

20. For the poor shall never cease out of the land; therefore I command thee saying, Thou shalt open thine hand wide unto thy brother, to thy poor and to thy needy in thy land. Deut. 15: 11.

21. And if thy brother an Hebrew man, or an Hebrew woman, be sold unto thee, and serve thee six years, then in the seventh year thou shalt let him go free from thee. And when thou sendest him out free from thee, thou shalt not let him go away empty. Deut. 15: 12.

22. Thou shalt furnish him liberally out of thy flock, and out of thy floor, and out of thy wine-

press; of that wherewith the Lord thy God hath blessed thee thou shalt give unto him. Deut. 15: 14.

23. It shall not seem hard unto thee, when thou sendest him away free from thee; for he hath been worth a double hired servant to thee, in serving thee six years; and the Lord thy God shall bless thee in all that thou doest. Deut. 15: 18.

24. Thou shalt not deliver unto his master the servant which is escaped from his master unto thee; he shall dwell with thee, even among you, in that place which he shall choose, in one of thy gates, where it liketh him best; thou shalt not oppress him. Deut. 23: 15.

25. If a man be found stealing any of his brethren of the children of Israel, and maketh merchandize of him, or selleth him; then that thief shall die; and thou shalt put evil away from among you. Deut. 24: 7.

26. Thou shalt not oppress an hired servant that is poor and needy, Whether he be of thy brethren, or of thy strangers that are in thy land within thy gates; at his day thou shalt give him his hire, neither shall the sun go down upon it; for he is poor, and setteth his heart upon it; lest he cry against thee unto the Lord, and it be sin unto thee. Deut. 24: 14.

27. Thou shalt not pervert the judgment of the stranger, nor of the fatherless, nor take the widows raiment to pledge; but thou shalt remember, that thou wast a bond-man in Egypt, and the Lord thy God redeemed the thence; therefore I command thee to do this thing. Deut. 24: 17.

NOTES ON CHAPTER II.

1. *If thou buy a Hebrew servant.*

Slavery existed among the neighboring nations of the Jews before this law was made, and the same reasons may be given for their being thus permitted to buy slaves, (not to steal them, nor, indeed, to buy those who had been stolen) which may be assigned for their being permitted to have a number of wives, and to kill those who murdered their nearest relations. But then, a Hebrew thus bought, could not be retained in slavery, (if such his condition might be called,) more than six years. And yet, how often we hear persons of the present age, appealing to this very law, as a justification of a system of slavery, which holds parents and their children in the very worst kind of bondage, from one generation to another, time without end!

2. *If a man sell his daughter.*

"This the Jews allowed no man to do," says Dr. A. Clarke, on this place, "but in extreme distress, when he had no goods, either moveable or immoveable left, even to the clothes on his back; and he had this permission only while she was *unmarriagable.* It may appear at first view strange, that such a law should have been given; but let it be remembered, that this servitude, could extend at the utmost, only to six years; and that it was nearly the same as in some cases of *apprenticeship* among us; where the parents *bind* the child for *seven years,* and have from his master so much for work during that time."

3. *He shall be sold for his theft.*

And how many slave masters in this nation, would now have to be sold themselves into slavery, were they to be judged by this law!

4. *He shall be surely punished.*

And here is another feature of the Mosaic law, in relation to servants, which shows how unjust and cruel that system of slavery is, which prevails in this land; among the Jews, if a servant was killed by the cruel treatment of his master, that master was punished with death. See Gen. 9:5. *Whoso shedeth man's blood, by man shall his blood be shed.* But not so now among us; in the United States, scores and hundreds of slaves have been killed by the treatment of their "masters" and "drivers," and not a single instance was ever known here, of a white man's being hung for the murder of a slave! And yet, these very persons refer us to this passage of Scripture, as a justification of slave-holding, because it is added, *notwithstanding, if he remain a day or two, he shall not be punished, for he is his money.* That is, if the servant servive a day or two after he had been deservedly beaten by his master, and then died, it might be presumed in that case, that he died from some other cause, and consequently the only punishment which the master should suffer was the loss of the servant's time, for the servant was to him, for the time being, instead of money. This passage is far from asserting that the servant was his master's property, in the same sense in which slaves are supposed to be the master's property, by the enslavers of this country; the sense of it, is simply, the servant, is to his master, instead of money, he represents, for the time being, his masters money.

5. *He shall surely be put to death.*

And would American, *Christian* enslavers be willing to be judged by this law? And is there one solitary slave-holder, in this nation, who, according to this precept, is not either, a man-thief, or a receiver of those who have been stolen? It does not and cannot alter the case, as to the manner in which one has come into the possession of those human beings whom he claims as his property; if they are found in his hand, this law says he should be put to death.

6. *I will surely hear their cry.*

The people of this land once felt themselves oppressed by the government of Great Britian. At that time they were comparatively poor and defenceless; but they cried unto the LORD and entreated Him to undertake for them; and now, the most skeptical acknowledge, that God did hear their cries and that He did undertake for them, against those who oppressed them. And now, who can read these words, and think of the millions of poor slaves who are so cruelly oppressed by this nation, and not tremble in view of the dangers to which it must, according to the principles of God's government, be exposed! Are there no orphan children, no afflicted widows, among our millions of slaves, whose cries God, in justice, may yet hear? And was it in answer to the cries of such, and in fulfillment of the threatening here denounced, that he permitted the dreadful scenes which occurred at Southampton, in Virginia, a few years ago?

7. *Neither deal falsely, neither lie one to another.*

The following fact may be given for thousands of the kind, which are constantly occurring among the enslavers of the human species; it is from the Hudson (Ohio) Observer; and it is said to have taken place not long since. "Mr. R. a public officer, boarding at the same place with myself, is a slave-holder, and a strong advocate for slavery. He came home a few days since and related the following circumstances.

"The Rev. Mr. B. is the owner of several slaves, one of which has a wife that belongs to another man in the city. The slave had been guilty of some crime and was confined in jail; and the Rev. Mr. B. came to me, not more than half an hour after preaching a funeral sermon, and offered to sell him to me. I went to the jail, with Mr. —— a noted slave-trader, to see the slave, and then returned and closed the bargain with the Rev. Mr. B., his master. 'Now,' said Mr. B. 'do not tell the slave, that you have bought him, but that I have let him out to you.' No, said I, I shall tell him no lies. We then went again to the jail, and Rev. Mr. B. said to the negro, 'Robert, I have hired you out to this man for a time, you must go with him.'

"But Robert, suspecting the horrid truth, from his having been just before examined by the slave-dealer, looked up to Mr. B. and said, — 'No, you have sold me to go down the river. Now, Mr. B.' he continued, ' you profess to be a Christian and a preacher of the gospel, *but how do you expect to get to heaven when you will sell me from my wife, to be sent down the river?* '" Here this preaching slave-holder, and slave-dealer, tells a lie himself, and attempts also to induce his neighbor to tell another, and all this in addition to his crime of having sold for money the *image* of the infinite God, and parted forever, a husband from his wife!

8. *The wages of him that is hired.*

If it was a sin against God, for one under the Mosaic economy to retain the wages of a hired servant for the space of one night only, how much more guilty must one be now, under the gospel dispensation, who compels a man to work during his whole life time, and pays him nothing for his hire?

9. *A stumbling-block before the blind.*

And is it no *crime* in the sight of a Holy God, to MAKE *millions* of human beings BLIND, as the slaves in this country are made, by the unjust and oppressive laws which forbid their instruction, even in a Sabbath school? This the laws of Louisiana do under the penalty of *five hundred dollars fine* for the first offence, and *death* for the second!

10. *Love thy neighbor as thyself.*

Do those who *violently withhold* their neighbors' *liberty* from them, love their neighbor AS themselves? And how near do those come to the fulfilling of this command, who sell husbands and part them forever from their wives? Who sell children and part them forever from their parents? Do those love their neighbors AS themselves, who take the avails of their labor without paying them for it?

11. *Thou shalt relieve him.*

No class of men in the known world, suffer a greater amount of evils than the slaves of this country; but from what part of these evils, the slave-holders or their apologists, are now endeavoring to relieve them, it is not very easy to determine. See Chap. I. and 6.

12. *Thou shalt not compel him to serve as a bond-servant.*

No Hebrew could be compelled to serve his master, more than six years, but a bond servant, that is, one who was not an Hebrew, might be compelled to serve till the year of Jubilee. A Hebrew might be retained in servitude till the year of Jubilee, if it was his own choice, not otherwise. See Ex. 21: 5, 6. Nor, indeed, could a Hebrew, nor any stranger, be retained in servitude any time, after he was abused and treated with unjustifiable severity by his master. See Ex. 21: 26, 27. Are all slaves in this land, set free as soon as they are maimed by their masters or drivers?

Every seventh day among the Jews was a Sabbath, or day of rest; every seventh year was also a Sabbath year, during which the land and the people rested, and all Hebrew servants were at liberty to go free from their masters. And then every fiftieth year was termed a Jubilee, beyond which time no servant could be held to the service of his master. See Chap. iv. 11.

13. *Of them shall ye buy bond-men and bond-maids.*

This the Jews might do by God's permission; and it was only by His permission, that they might buy one of their own nation for a servant; and hence it follows, that for any people to do this now, without God's permission, is really as sinful as it would be for them to commence an offensive and exterminating war against a

*3

neighboring nation. And it should always be borne in mind, in the examination of this subject, that, though the ancient Hebrews were permitted to buy servants and keep them for a limited time; yet they were never authorized to *steal* them, or to buy or keep those who had been *stolen*. And it is certain, the Jews were suffered to do some things which it is not lawful nor consistent for Christians to do, of the present age; hence, Christ said, *Moses because of the hardness of your hearts, suffered you to put away your wives; but from the beginning it was not so.* Matt. 19: 8.

14. *Ye shall be remembered.*

Here God promised the Jews success, when they went to war against those who oppressed them; would not the same principles of his government lead him to favor the oppressed in this land, in an attempt to gain their freedom? At the same time, no Christian, who is opposed to slavery, would, or could for one moment, either propose or encourage such an attempt, otherwise than in the use of moral means. The true friends of the enslaved in this land, do not believe it would be right, for the oppressed to use any violence, (not even the whips with which their own backs have been so often lacerated) for the purpose of obtaining their rights. Yet, should the slaves ever attempt this by any means, says the immortal Jefferson, "The Almighty has no attribute which could take sides with us in such a contest."

15. *Thou shalt not steal.*

This commandment would certainly have prevented all slaveholding among the Jews, had it not been for the express permission of God; just the same as the command which says, *Thou shalt not kill*, would have prevented the nearest of kin, among the Jews, from killing the murderer of his friend, without a process at law, if God had not given them his permission to do this.

Now, here is a man who holds in his possession the liberty of one of his species; it is the liberty of a slave, who was born in his own house; this slave never gave this master his liberty, he never sold it to him, nor has he ever forfeited it by crime, but yet the master has got it in his possession, and he holds it fast. How come this master by the liberty of this man? He never bought it of the slave, and the slave could not have sold it, if he would; nor has he bought it of a third person, for it never was possessed by a third person. How came he by it, if he did not steal it? We know, indeed, it may be said, that the laws gave the master a title to this man's liberty; but who made those laws? Why slaveholders, to be sure! And where did slaveholders obtain their authority to make laws, which controvene the law of the infinite God, which says, *Thou shalt not steal?* The truth is, they have no such authority, they never had, and they never can have; and hence every man who holds the person of a human being as his *property*, does so in violation of the eighth commandment, which says, *Thou shalt not steal!*

But suppose again, that the liberty of this slave is sold to a third person; is the man's title, to the liberty of this enslaved human being, any better than his who sells it? Does not the purchaser know, as every man in this nation knows, that this man has been robbed of his liberty, — that he never has been, and that he never can be paid an equivalent for it? And yet, he buys and holds in his possession that which he knows has been stolen, and to which he cannot have, in the nature of things, any just title! Now let the reader suppose a case, if he can, of one slave in this land whose liberty has not been stolen, and which is not now withheld by an act of fraud, and theft, similar to that stated above.

Neither shalt thou covet anything that is thy neighbor's.

And how can one withhold from his neighbor, his *personal* LIBERTY, his *wife*, his *children*, and *keep back the fruit of his labor*, and not break this command of God? And yet, I once heard this very precept quoted in the Theological Seminary at Andover, to prove that slavery must continue to exist to the end of time, or this commandment, it was supposed, could not be fulfilled! So persecution must continue to the end of the world, or Christians cannot have the privilege of praying for their persecutors! And human intelligences must always continue in a course of sin, or the Deity will not have the glory of forgiving them!

And it be sin unto thee.

And think you not, reader, that there are a few Christian enslavers in this land, who need to have these and the foregoing cautions repeated in their hearing? Mark how strictly the Jews were commanded to remember and *pity* the *poor*, the *fatherless* and *widows*; and to give them sufficient for their need, in that which they might want for their souls and their bodies. And is the great

God less merciful, less just, less jealous now, for the welfare of the *poor slave?*

19. *Thou shalt surely give him, — and thy heart shall not be grieved when thou givest unto him.*

We not unfrequently hear of the liberal gifts which many enslavers bestow for the advancement of some particular objects; but how seldom does ever one slave have his liberty restored to him, and how seldom do any of them receive anything like a just equivalent for their toils and labors! If we request those who have grown rich and fed upon the slave's unrequited labor ever since they were born, to restore to the injured slave his rights, without even making any *gift* to him at all, their hearts are "grieved" at once, and we are told, that we are only rendering the slave's condition worse, than it was before, by making such a request!

21. *Thou shalt not let him go away empty.*

This was a matter of *justice*. From this and the following passages, it appears, that in six years, a servant among the Hebrews, brought a sufficient profit to his master to pay him double for his freedom, and to furnish himself with grain and stock to begin to labor for his own support. How will the conduct of the slave-masters in this land, who refuse ever, to let their servants go free at all, and who perpetually withhold from them all remuneration for their labors, compare with this law?

24. *Thou shalt not deliver unto his master, &c.*

This is supposed to refer to the case of a servant who had fled from an idolatrous master, and gone over to the children of Israel; if so, admitting the justice of the present system of slavery, would there not be precisely as much propriety in applying this passage to the cases of those slaves who now run away from their wicked and cruel masters, as there is in quoting other passages of Scripture to justify this system of slavery?

25. *That thief shall die.*

Many thousands of the people of color, who are legally free in this land, have been stolen, kidnapped, and sold into interminable, and hopeless bondage; and there is abundance of evidence which may be relied on to prove, that scores of such are stolen and sold into slavery in this country every year, besides the two hundred, or more who are seized and made slaves of, every day as soon as they are born. How will this law apply to these facts?

27. *Thou shalt remember that thou wast a bond-man in Egypt.*

And how can Americans forget the bondage which they once suffered, and from which they fought and bled to be free? Well has Jefferson exclaimed;— "What an incomprehensible machine is man! Who can endure toil, famine, stripes, imprisonment, and death itself, in vindication of his own liberty, and the next moment be deaf to all those motives whose power supported him through his trial, and inflict on his fellow men a bondage, one hour of which is fraught with more misery, than ages of that which he rose in rebellion to oppose."

"But," adds this truly great man, "We must wait with patience the workings of an overruling Providence, and hope that, that is preparing the deliverance of these our suffering brethren. When the measure of their tears shall be full, when their groans shall have involved heaven itself in darkness — doubtless a God of justice, will awaken to their distress, and by diffusing light and liberality among their *oppressors*, or at length by his exterminating thunder, manifest his attention to the things of this world, and that they are not left to the guidance of a blind fatality."

CHAPTER III.

JOSHUA, JOB AND EZRA.

God has always delivered His people from the oppression of their enemies, when they cried unto Him for deliverance.

1. And when the Lord raised them up Judges, then the Lord was with the judge, and delivered them out of the hand of their enemies all the days

of the judge: for it repented the LORD because of their groanings by reason of them that oppressed them and vexed them. Jud. 2: 18.

2. Thus saith the LORD God of Israel, I brought you up from Egypt, and brought you forth out of the house of bondage; and I delivered you out of the hand of the Egyptians, and out of the hand of all that oppressed you, and drave them out from before you and gave you their land. Jud. 6: 8.

3. The Zidonians also and the Amalekites and the Maonites did oppress you; and ye cried to me, and I delivered you out of their hand. Jud. 10: 12.

4. Now therefore ye are cursed, and there shall none of you be freed from being bondmen, and hewers of wood and drawers of water, for the house of my God. Josh. 9: 23.

5. There the wicked cease from troubling, and there the weary be at rest. There the prisoners rest together; they hear not the voice of the oppressor. The small and the great are there; and the servant is free from his master. Job, 3: 17.

6. To him that is afflicted pity should be showed from his friend. Job. 6: 14.

7. The wicked man travaileth in pain all his days, and the number of days is hidden to the oppressor. A dreadful sound is in his ears; in prosperity the destroyer shall come upon him. Job, 15: 20.

8. Because he hath oppressed and hath forsaken the poor; because he hath violently taken away an house which he builded not, surely he shall not feel quietness in his belly, he shall not save of that which he desired. Job, 20: 19.

9. This is the portion of a wicked man with

God, and the heritage of oppressors, which they shall recieve of the Almighty. Job, 27 : 13

10. When the ear heard me then it blessed me, and when the eye saw me, it gave witness to me; because I delivered the poor that cried, and the fatherless and him that had none to help him. The blessing of him that was ready to perish came upon me : and I caused the widows heart to sing for joy. Job 29 : 11.

11. I was eyes to the blind, and feet was I to the lame. I was a father to the poor ; and the cause which I knew not, I searched out. Job 29 : 15.

12. If I did dispise the cause of my man-servant, or of my maid-servant, when they contended with me ; what then shall I do when God riseth up? And when he visiteth, what shall I answer him? Job 31 : 13.

13. If I have withheld the poor from their desire, or have caused the eyes of the widow to fail ; or have eaten my morsel myself alone, and the fatherless hath not eaten thereof; if I have seen any perish for want of clothing, or any poor without covering, if his loins have not blessed me, and if he were not warmed with the fleece of my sheep ; if I have lifted up my hand against the fatherless, when I saw my help in the gate ; then let mine arm fall from my shoulder blade, and mine arm be broken from the bone. Job 31 : 16.

14. By reason of the multitude of oppressions, they make the oppressed to cry ; they cry out by reason of the arm of the mighty. Job 35 : 9.

15. He delivereth the poor in his affliction, and openeth their ears in oppression. Job 36 : 15.

16. And now for a little space grace hath been

showed from the Lord our God, to leave us a remnant to escape, and to give us a nail in his holy place, that our God may lighten our eyes, and give us a little reviving in our bondage. Ezra 9 : 8.

NOTES ON CHAPTER III.

1. *Them that oppressed them.*

The Jews were delivered into the hands of their enemies, not unfrequently, as a chastisement for their sins ; yet, even in these cases, God regarded their groanings, and when they cried unto him, he saved them from the power of their oppressors. But the bondage which the slaves of this land are now suffering, is not a punishment for any sin which they can have committed ; they are guilty of no crime either against God or man, for which they are now enslaved ; and hence, there is so much the more reason to believe, that when they cry unto the Great Avenger of wrongs, He will hear, and deliver them.

2. *And gave you their land.*

And will not this language apply with some degree of propriety to the people of this nation ? Have we not been delivered from the hand of the oppressor ? Do we not now inherit the land that once belonged to others ? And shall we now, in our turn, become the *oppressors* of the poor and defenceless ? It is a remarkable fact, that this nation does now oppress a greater number of its own citizens, by the system of slavery which it upholds, than the whole number of our forefathers who were oppressed formerly by the government of Great Britian ! Yes, a greater number of the citizens of these United States, are now far more cruelly oppressed by our own government, than our ancestors were who rose in rebellion sixty years ago against the government of England ; and one hour of that bondage which we now inflict on three millions of our own citizens, as Jefferson remarks, is fraught with more misery and guilt, than ages of that which we rose in rebellion to oppose !

3. *Ye cried to me, and I delivered you.*

The oppression here referred to, as remarked above, was what the Jews suffered as a chastisement for their sins ; and yet God delivered them from it, as soon as they repented and cried unto him.

And is it presumption in us to infer, that God will now deliver the oppressed in answer to prayer, and especially such as have not sinned against him? Will not God hear his own people, who cry day and night unto him, in the behalf of those that are in bonds, and who have committed no crime?

4. *Ye are cursed.*

This, as the reader will have perceived, refers to the Gibeonites; they were among the nations whom the Hebrews were commanded utterly to destroy for their idolatry. Deut. 20: 17. But by stratagems and lies, they so deceived Joshua, that he entered into a covenant with them, and gave them a solemn oath, that they should be spared. For this wicked deception, this curse was pronounced upon them, by which their national existence was annihilated. The state of servitude, to which these idolators were reduced, was a blessing to them, because without it they must have been put to death. And has God ever given a command to any of the people of this country, to commence a war of extermination against Africa, and to make slaves of all who are not put to death?

5. *The servant is free from his master.*

How often the weary, worn out slaves look to the grave as the place of their rest; and how many thousands of them must, in all probability, die without any well grounded hope of rest beyond it!

> " Let sorrow bathe each blushing cheek,
> Bend piteous o'er the tortured slave,
> Whose wrongs compassion cannot speak,
> Whose only refuge is the grave."

6. *Pity should be shown.*

But let a white man or woman at the South, manifest the least pity for the afflicted slaves, and it will be sure to bring down upon himself, the scorn and contempt of most of their " masters " and " drivers."

7. *A dreadful sound is in his ears.*

Or as the margin reads, a *sound of fear* is in his ears. This is said of the oppressor; and a more striking illustration of this truth, could not well be given, perhaps, than that made in a speech delivered in the house of delegates of Virginia, in January 1832, on the policy of the state with regard to her slave population, by James McDowell, Jr.

4

One of the members of the house had remarked, that the insurrection at Southampton, when scores of the whites had been murdered by the slaves, was a " petty affair; " upon which Mr. McDowell read extracts from a number of letters written by some of the most respectable men in the State, to show the terror and dismay which prevailed in the minds of the citizens in every part of the community, and then proceeded as follows:—

" Now, sir, I ask you, I ask gentlemen in conscience to say, was this a ' petty affair ? ' I ask you whether that was a ' petty affair,' which startled the feelings of your whole population — which threw a portion of it into alarm — a portion of it into panic; which wrung out from an affrighted people the thrilling cry, day after day conveyed to your executive, ' We are in peril of our lives, send us an army for defence.' Was that a ' petty affair ' which drove families from their homes, which assembled women and children in crowds, and without shelter, at places of common refuge, in every condition of weakness and infirmity, under every suffering which want, and pain, and terror could inflict, yet willing to endure all — willing to meet death from famine, death from climate, death from hardships, preferring anything rather than the horrors of meeting it from a domestic assassin ? Was that a ' petty affair ' which erected a peaceful and confiding portion of the State, into a military camp, which outlawed from pity the unfortunate beings whose brothers had offended, which barred every door, penetrated every bosom with fear or suspicion, which so banished every sense of security from every man's dwelling, that let but a hoof or a horn break upon the silence of the night, and an aching throb would be driven to the heart; the husband would look to his weapon, and the mother would shudder and weep upon her cradle!

" Was it the fear of Nat Turner, and his deluded drunken handful of fellows, which produced such effects ? Was it this that induced distant countries, where the very name of Southampton was strange, to arm and equip for a struggle ? No, sir, it was the *suspicion* eternally attached to the slave himself, the *suspicion* that a Nat Turner might be in every family, that the same bloody deed could be acted over at any time and in any place, that the materials for it were spread through the land and always ready for a like explosion. Nothing but the force of this *withering apprehension*, nothing but the paralyzing and deadening weight, with which it falls upon and prostrates the heart of every man who has helpless dependents to protect, nothing but this could have thrown a brave people into consternation, or could have made any portion of this powerful Commonwealth, for a single instant to have quailed and trembled."

Yes, it is the " withering apprehension," which every slaveholder in this land carries in his own conscience, that the slaves have been *outraged, insulted* and *wronged*, which makes *the sound of fear in his ears.*

8. *He shall not feel guiltless.*

How true it is, that no enslaver, in this land, *feels guiltless*, every person at all acquainted with the subject of slavery well knows. The remarks of Mr. McDowell show, that a general sense of danger and insecurity everywhere prevails to a great extent, in the slave-states. Hence the enslavers often go armed, and keep their arms constantly about their beds at night, for fear the slaves may rise and take vengeance upon those who have oppressed them.

9. *They shall receive of the Almighty.*

The evils described in the following verses, sometimes come upon tyrants, and such as oppress their fellow men, by the direction of God.

10. *The blessing of him that was ready to perish.*

And how very desirable is such a blessing! How much to be preferred before honors, or silver, or gold, or all that this world can afford! And let every friend of the oppressed, pray that it may come upon all the slave-holders in this, and every other part of the world!

11. *The cause which I knew not, I searched out.*

I spared neither time nor pains to find out the condition of the oppressed and afflicted, that I might afford them all possible relief. And is it not likely that some of Job's contemporaries reproached him with " meddling with that which did not concern him ? "

12. *If I did despise the cause of my servant.*

As though he had said :— I have not denied my servants any privilege, whether civil or religious, which I enjoyed myself; if they had any cause of complaint against any one, or even against myself, I gave them a candid and impartial hearing, and rendered a just judgment in the case. Can the Christian enslavers of this land say this, now, of themselves? And what will they do when God riseth up, if they have not done this?

13. *Then let mine arm fall from my shoulder-blade.*

This is a most solemn asseveration, that he never had wronged or oppressed the poor in any way, but that he had always administered to the wants of such, as far as it had been in his power. O that all who profess the Christian name, could now say this, with as much truth as it was said by this ancient patriarch!

14. *They cry out by reason of the arm of the mighty.*

The Rev. Mr. Gilgrass, one of the Wesleyan Missionaries, in the West Indies, relates the following fact. "A master who lived near us in Kingston, Jamaica, wanted some money; and one of his female slaves having two fine children, he sold one of them, and the child was torn from her maternal affection. In the agony of her feelings, she made a hideous *howling ;* and for that crime was flogged. Soon after he sold her other child. This 'turned her heart within her,' and impelled her into a kind of madness. She *howled* night and day in the yard, tore her hair, ran up and down the streets and the parade, rending the heavens with her *cries,* and literally watering the earth with her tears. Her constant cry was, '*Da wicked massa Jew, he sell me children. Will no buckra massa pity nega? What me do? Me have no child.*' As she stood before my window, she lifted up her hands towards heaven, and said:—' *My massa, do me massa minister pity me! Me heart do so* (shaking herself violently) *me heart do so, because me have no child ; me go a massa house, in massa yard, and in me hut, and me no see em!*'"

15. *He openeth their ears in oppression.*

He gives them instruction and comfort notwithstanding their chains, when they look unto God for it. The Infinite Being is the great author and patron of *science,* nor can there scarcely be a more flagrant sin against Him, than to prevent the *instruction* of the IMMORTAL MINDS whom He has made, and which He has endowed with a deathless capacity, and an insatiable thirst for the lights of science and religion.

And yet in this *republican* this *Christian* land, we have numerous laws made and sanctioned with the heaviest penalties which it is in the power of human governments to inflict, for the very purpose of putting out the eyes of the mind, for the very purpose of preventing the instruction of millions of the citizens of these free and independent States! In view of this *one* appalling fact, what

American will not "tremble for his country, when he reflects that God is just!"

CHAPTER IV.

DAVID.

God has always manifested a peculiar pity and regard for the oppressed — and he promises his blessing upon all such as imitate Him in this thing.

1. LORD, thou hast heard the desire of the humble: thou wilt prepare their heart, thou wilt cause thine ear to hear; to judge the fatherless and the oppressed, that the men of the earth may no more oppress. Ps. 10: 17.

2. When he maketh inquisition for blood, he remembereth them; he forgetteth not the cry of the humble. Ps. 9: 12.

3. For the oppression of the poor, for the sighing of the needy, now will I arise, saith the LORD; I will set him in safety from him that puffeth at him. Ps. 12: 5.

4. For he hath not despised nor abhorred the affliction of the afflicted, neither hath he hid his face from him; but when he cried unto him he heard. Ps. 22: 24.

5. Blessed is he that considereth the poor; the LORD will deliver him in time of trouble. The

Lord will preserve him, and keep him alive; and he shall be blessed upon the earth; and thou wilt not deliver him unto the will of his enemies. The Lord will strengthen him upon the bed of languishing; thou wilt make all his bed in his sickness. Ps. 41: 1.

6. The Lord will command his loving kindness in the day time, and in the night his song shall be with me, and my prayer unto the God of my life. I will say unto God my rock, Why hast thou forgotten me? Why go I mourning because of the oppression of the enemy? Ps. 42: 8.

7. But unto the wicked, God saith, What hast thou to do, to declare my statutes, or that thou shouldst take my covenant in thy mouth? seeing thou hatest instruction, and castest my words behind thee. When thou sawest a thief, then thou consentedst with him, and hast been partaker with adulterers. Ps. 50: 16.

8. Give the king thy judgments, O God, and thy righteousness unto the king's son. He shall judge the poor of the people, he shall save the children of the needy, and shall break in pieces the oppressor. Ps. 72: 1.

9. For he shall deliver the needy when he crieth; the poor also, and him that hath no helper. He shall spare the poor and needy, and shall save the souls of the needy. He shall redeem their soul from deceit and violence; and precious shall their blood be in his sight. Ps. 72: 12.

10. Defend the poor and fatherless; do justice to the afflicted and needy. Deliver the poor and needy; rid them out of the hand of the wicked. Ps. 82: 3.

11. Blessed is the people that know the joyful

sound; they shall walk, O Lord, in the light of thy countenance; in thy name shall they rejoice all the day; and in thy righteousness shall they be exalted. Ps. 89: 15.

12. The Lord executeth righteousness and judgment for all that are oppressed. Ps. 103: 6.

13. Deliver me from the oppression of man, so will I keep thy precepts. Ps. 119: 134.

14. I know that the Lord will maintain the cause of the afflicted, and the right of the poor. Ps. 140: 12.

15. The Lord looseth the prisoners; the Lord openeth the eyes of the blind; the Lord raiseth them that are bowed down; the Lord loveth the righteous; the Lord preserveth the strangers; he relieveth the fatherless and widow; but the way of the wicked he turneth upside down. Ps. 146: 7.

NOTES ON CHAPTER IV.

1. *Thou wilt prepare their heart.*

Thou wilt give them a disposition to seek after thee. So the great and good Being often sheds light upon the dark mind of the poor slave, who is oppressed, notwithstanding the unjust and cruel laws which are enacted to keep him in darkness. And when the heart of the afflicted is thus prepared, God hears the prayer which they offer unto Him.

2. *He forgetteth not the cry of the humble.*

Let no one be discouraged in praying for the deliverance and salvation of the enslaved; God may seem not to hear for a while, but the prayer of faith shall not be forgotten, it shall be answered in due time. God remembers, not only the oppressed, but also those who make inquisition for their blood. The following account of some of the bloody inquisitions of this land, is from the pen of Dr. J. Torry of Philadelphia. He says;—

"Thomas Clarkson states, in his History of the Abolition of the Slave-Trade, that the arrival of slave-ships, on the coasts of Africa, was the uniform signal for the immediate commencement of wars for the attainment of prisoners, for sale and exportation to America and the West Indies. In Maryland and Delaware, the same drama is now performed in miniature. The arrival of the *Man-Traffickers*, laden with cash, at their respective stations near the coasts, or at their several *inland posts*, near the dividing line of Maryland and Delaware, (at some of which they have great prisons for the purpose) is the well known signal for the professed *kidnappers*, like beasts of prey, to commence their nightly invasions upon the fleecy flocks; extending their ravages, (generally attended with bloodshed and sometimes with murder,) and spreading terror and consternation, among both freemen and slaves, throughout the sandy regions, from the western to the eastern shores. These *blood-hounds* when overtaken, which is rare, by the messengers of the law, are generally found armed with instruments of death, sometimes with pistols with patent spring daggers attached to them." In this way, thousands of innocent unoffending men women and children, have been stolen and carried from their friends and homes in this land of boasted freedom, and themselves and posterity doomed to suffer all the horrors of an unending bondage.

3. *Now will I arise, saith the Lord.*

With such promises as this, the Bible abounds; and as sure as God is true, so surely He will yet undertake for the oppressed. At the same time, we should keep in view, his long-suffering and patience towards the oppressor; He pities these also, and commands them to repent, and it becomes our duty to pity them, and pray for them accordingly.

4. *He hath not despised — the affliction of the afflicted.*

The poor and the afflicted are generally despised, by those who are the cause of the evils which they suffer; but the affliction of the oppressed is not despised by the Great God.

5. *Considereth the poor.*

By finding out their condition, visiting them, and administering to their wants. As a most remarkable example of this kind, let the reader consult the life of John Howard, and he will perceive how strictly the promise was fulfilled, which is made here to those who perform this heavenly work.

6. *Why hast thou forgotten me?*

This inquiry the Psalmist was sometimes led to make, when he was in trouble; and when we reflect, for a moment, upon the accumulated wrongs which millions of the population of this country are doomed to suffer by the slave-system, can we wonder that some of them should adopt this language? Is it a marvelous thing, that many of them should be tempted to think, that there is no God of justice? — That their masters, who profess to love Him, and their fellow men as themselves, are hypocrites?

7. *Thou consentedst with him.*

And by what process of reasoning can it be shown, that every slave-holder in this land, does not, in some sense, countenance the conduct of the adulterer and the man-thief? The man who makes a habit of using intoxicating liquors, even if it be ever so temperately, is now set down by the voice of nearly the whole Christian world, as countenancing and promoting the cause of intemperance; and if he be a professed Christian or Christian minister, his example is believed and known to be so much the more pernicious and fatal in its influence. For who does not know, that the unprincipled, intemperate rum-drinker, does invariably refer to the habit of the very good Christian, who uses the liquid poison, as a sufficient justification of his intemperance?

And the more good which may be said of such a professing Christian, in some respects, the more dependence will be placed, by the intemperate, upon his example. And it is precisely so of the very *kind* and *Christian enslavers* of the human species; they do the very same to perpetuate the crime and the evils of slave-holding, which the respectable and Christian rum-drinker, or the Christian distiller, does, to perpetuate the evils of intemperance. And it is remarkable, that the most conclusive argument which can be adduced at the present day, in favor of slave-holding, under any circumstances, is the fact, that both *Christians* and *Christian ministers*, nay some of the most *kind*, and *respectable* people at the South and West, are SLAVE-HOLDERS!!! Now can any candid observer fail of seeing, that these very *respectable*, *kind*, and *Christian* ENSLAVERS *of the human species*, stand just as much in the way of the final abolition of slavery and the domestic slave-trade in this country, as the *respectable* and *Christian* DISTILLERS and RUM-DRINKERS, do in the way of the temperance reformation?

How frequently the opposers of slavery are now tauntingly asked, "Why do you not send your agents to the South, where slavery exists?" We answer, for the very same reason that temperance agents do not spend their strength in preaching to the *intemperate*. We know that all successful action in the Anti-slavery cause, as well as in the temperance cause, must be carried on by those who are not " partakers with " such as commit the evils which it is intended to remove.

8. *He shall break in pieces the oppressor.*

This is said of Christ; and so far as Christianity has prevailed in other civilized countries, it has already annihilated slavery, and broken the iron arm of the oppressor.

10. *Deliver the poor.*

We shall see in the course of these chapters, that there are as many commands in the Bible to a third person, to deliver the oppressed out of the hand of the oppressor, as there are commands to the oppressor, to let the oppressed go free.

11. *The joyful sound.*

The sound of the trumpet, on the morning of the first day of the jubilee. *Then shalt thou cause the trumpet of the Jubilee to sound, on the tenth day of the seventh month, on the day of atonement, shall ye make the trumpet to sound throughout all your land, And ye shall hallow the fiftieth year, and proclaim liberty throughout all the land unto* ALL THE INHABITANTS *thereof; it shall be a jubilee unto you; and ye shall return every man unto his possession, and ye shall return every man unto his family.* Lev. 25: 9. Hence it appears, that on the arrival of this joyful day, *all the inhabitants* of the land of Judea, were *free*, and every one received again his forfeited or lost possessions.

13 *So, will I keep thy precepts.*

Hence the *sin* of *oppression;* it incapacitates the oppressed from obeying all the precepts of God. How can those females in this land fulfill, or how may they be expected to fulfill, all of God's commands, when they are not permitted to read them, and when they have no protection, either in the laws or in public sentiment, for their purity or persons? They may be compelled to submit to the beastly lusts of any white man, by the stroke of the cow-hide, or to avoid death, without the possibility of any redress! How can those slaves who are husbands, (in the sight of God) and who are fathers also, fulfill that command which makes it their duty to love their wives and provide for their families, when they are torn from their wives and children, and sold into a distant part of the country? The command of God makes it their duty to bring up their children "in the knowledge and discipline of God," but they are not suffered either to read the Bible themselves, or to teach their children to read it! God commands all children to honor their parents, and obey them in the Lord, but the children of more than a million of parents in this land, are prohibited, and *hindered* from doing this, by the laws of the states where they live; and the same laws prohibit all colored persons, whether slaves or free, from worshipping God according to the dictates of their own consciences. The statutes of Virginia ordain, that any free person of color, whether ordained or not, for preaching or exhorting at any religious meeting, may be siezed by any person *without a warrant*, and punished with *thirty-nine lashes;* and any free person of color attending such a meeting may be seized and punished in a like manner. Similar laws are in force in the other slave-states; so true it is, that civil and religious liberty generally stand or fall together.

CHAPTER V.

SOLOMON.

God has threatened his displeasure against all such as forbear to deliver the poor and the needy from the hands of those who oppress them.

1. The poor is hated even of his own neighbor; but the rich hath many friends. He that despiseth his neighbor sinneth; but he that hath mercy on the poor, happy is he. Prov. 14: 20.

2. He that oppresseth the poor reproacheth his maker; but he that honoreth him hath mercy on the poor. Prov. 14: 31.

3. He that oppresseth the poor to increase his riches, and he that giveth to the rich shall surely come to want. Prov. 22: 16.

4. Rob not the poor because he is poor; neither oppress the afflicted in the gate; for the LORD will plead their cause, and spoil the soul of those that spoiled them. Prov. 22: 22.

5. Remove not the old landmark; and enter not into the fields of the fatherless; for their Redeemer is mighty; he shall plead their cause with thee. Prov. 23: 10.

6. If thou forbear to deliver them that are drawn unto death, and those that are ready to be slain; if thou sayest, Behold, we knew it not; doth not he that pondereth the heart consider it? and he that keepeth thy soul, doth he not know it? and shall not he render to every man according to his works? Prov. 24: 11.

7. The righteous considereth the cause of the poor; but the wicked regardeth not to know it. Prov. 29: 7.

8. Open thy mouth for the dumb, in the cause of all such as are appointed to destruction. Open thy mouth, judge righteously, and plead the cause of the poor and needy. Prov. 31: 8.

9. So I returned and considered all the oppressions that are done under the sun; and, behold, the tears of such as were oppressed, and they had no comforter; and on the side of their oppressors there was power; but they had no comforter. Eccl. 4: 1.

10. If thou seest the oppression of the poor, and

violent perverting of judgment and justice in a province, marvel not at the matter; for he that is higher than the highest regardeth, and there be higher than they. Eccl. 5: 8.

11. Surely oppression maketh a wise man mad; and a gift destroyeth the heart. Eccl. 7: 7.

12. All the brethren of the poor do hate him; how much more do his friends go far from him; he pursueth them with words, yet they are wanting to him. Prov. 19: 7.

13. Better is a little with righteousness, than great revenues without right. Prov. 16: 8.

NOTES ON CHAPTER V.

1. *Hated even of his own neighbor.*

Are not the enslavers of this land the *neighbors* of those whom they enslave? Are they not indebted to the slaves for their living, and in fact, generally, all the substance they possess? And yet who hates the slave and the race of which they form a part, if the enslavers do not?

He that despiseth his neighbor, sinneth.

Hence it is clearly proved, that to indulge any kind of *prejudice* against one who has committed no crime, merely because he is poor, or differs from us in complexion, is a sin against God; and this sin becomes the more aggravating as it deprives him of any of the rights or privileges to which he is entitled by the dictates of reason and religion.

2. *Reproacheth his Maker.*

The poor are Christ's representatives on earth; and if it is a sin against God to despise and oppress one who is poor in the ordinary course of Providence, or one who has become so through some unavoidable calamity, how much more wicked must it be to *make men poor* by *oppressing* them? Surely if it is a sin and a reproach against God, to oppress such as are already poor, it must be a greater sin and more of an insult to the infinite Being, to make men poor, and to enact laws and enforce them for the very purpose of keeping them, not only poor, but, degraded and ignorant.

3. *To increase his riches.*

And for what other purpose are the poor slaves oppressed and kept in bondage, but to increase the masters' riches? But it is really difficult for one who never was " a broker in the trade of blood," to determine, how any man, especially, how any Christian, can enjoy the riches which he knows were earned by others, under the stroke of the cart-whip, perhaps, and by those too, who were never paid one penny as an equivalent for their labors!

4. *Because he is poor.*

It is because the slaves are poor and unable to assert and defend their rights, that their masters compel them to labor, and then take the fruits of their unrequited toil. This, God calls, *robbing them because they are poor;* and shall we call it by any other name?

Neither oppress the afflicted in the gate.

Courts of justice were usually held in the gates of cities in the east; hence the text means, that the poor and afflicted should have a fair and impartial hearing when they appeared at the court for judgment in any case.

In twelve of these United States, no person of color, whether male or female can be heard as an evidence in a court of justice against a white person. And another law which is general among the slave-states, prevents the slave or any person for him, from commencing a suit at law in certain cases, unless he first give security for the costs of court, and if the action should be tried and should fail, the costs are *doubled!* If this be not *oppressing the poor in the gate,* reader, what is?

Here is a " master," who, for some slight offence, strikes the child of a slave, in the presence of fifty other persons of color, who are slaves, and who see the " master " inflict the blow which causes the instant death of the child. But for the parents who look on and see their offspring gasp in death, there is *no redress;* the deed not being witnessed by any white person, it is passed over in silence, and so, indeed, such atrocities often are, when they occur under the eye of the whites. A slave may be compelled to see the person of his daughter or wife abused, as they often are, without being suffered to speak one word, or to move a finger in their defence. And will not the Great God plead the cause of such?

5. *He shall plead their cause.*

The slavery system now, has many excuses and apologies made for it; but there is not one among them all, but which any Christian would be ashamed to make at the judgment of the great day. But when God pleads the cause of the oppressed, who will answer him, then?

6. *We knew it not.*

And how many thousands say thus at the present day, in reference to the slaves of this land who are drawn unto death. "We are not enslavers, — we know not what the condition of the slave is — we don't live at the south — what have we to do with the subject?" Answer, —

1. If we do not know what the moral and political condition of nearly three million of slaves is, in this land, we are in fault, because, we may know, and we ought to know; nor indeed, will God consider it a sufficient excuse for the neglect of our duty when we say, *we knew it not.*

2. If we are not enslavers ourselves, we are *partakers of the sins* of those who are slave-holders, unless we set our faces against it, and use our utmost Christian-like endeavors to deliver the enslaved.

3. Our not living at the South, or indeed in America, is not a sufficient reason why we should do nothing to deliver those that are *ready to be slain* in this country. We do not live in Africa, and shall we do nothing to Christianize and civilize that country on this account? Though, by the way, it is acknowledged, that before we can do anything *consistently*, as a *Christian* people, for that nation, we should liberate her children whom we now keep in *chains*, and give them the Bible and all the other blessings which Christianity is designed to confer upon the world.

7. *Regardeth not to know it.*

How truly characteristic this is of many, very many, Christian ministers, and rulers in this nation, with regard to the wrongs of the poor slaves! They would be glad not to know them; they feel so much reluctance against saying or doing anything upon the subject. And who would not like to be ignorant upon this subject, if his ignorance would annihilate slavery from the nation, and from the world?

8. *Open thy mouth for the dumb.*

The slaves of this land are *dumb*, in a most affecting sense, inasmuch as they never have been, and are not now permitted to speak for themselves; and how can any Christian or Christian minister, neglect the duty which God here enjoins upon him in relation to these human beings ! And this, too, when he knows, that they are made and kept *poor* and *needy* by the bondage which they are violently compelled to endure !

9. *I considered all the oppressions.*

The Hebrew, *ashakim*, here rendered *oppressions*, signifies all those kinds of *injustice* or *injury* which one can suffer in his *person, prepertу*, or *character*. To withhold from a man his personal liberty, to compel him to labor without giving him any just equivalent for his labors, is to injure him in his person, property and character, this is robbery and oppression in their very worst forms.

On the side of their oppressors there was power.

The enslavers of this land have, *law*, and *prejudice*, and *riches* on their side; these are indeed powerful. But all these together, cannot withstand the arm of omnipotence, when God shall arise to plead the cause of the oppressed.

And is it not true, that the slaves have *no comforter* ? Who is permitted to pour into their desponding hearts the consolations of hope, or the balm of God's promises ? Let the following extract from the laws of Louisiana say, who ?

"If any person in Louisiana, from the *box*, *bench*, *stage*, *pulpit*, or any other place, or in *convsrsation*, shall make use of any *language*, *signs*, or *actions* having a *tendency* to produce discontent among free colored people, or insubordination among the slaves [such as may give them a hope in the promise of God, that, they shall be free] such person shall be punished with *imprisonment* from *three* to *twenty-one years*, or with DEATH, at the discretion of the court.''

And this is but a transcript of similar laws which are in force in nearly all of the slave-states. *Twenty-one years' imprisonment* or *death* upon the gallows, for speaking one word, or happening to make some kind of a *jesture* which may be *interpreted* as having a *tendency* to cause certain acts !!! Was the like ever heard of before, in the annals of the whole world !!

And yet, as often as we quote the word of God, or attempt to say anything against these most cruel and wicked of all laws that were ever passed by any government since the world began, we must be asked in scorn, " Why do you not go into those states where slavery exists and labor for its overthrow?" And those persons who so tauntingly make this inquiry, are "opposed to slavery," they tell us! Very well, and if they are opposed to it, pray, why do *they* not go into the slave states and tell the people, that they are opposed to slavery, and not tarry here, at the north and oppose all that others are striving to do for the removal of this great and growing evil? If they are, indeed, willing to be *fined, imprisoned for twenty-one years*, or to be *hung* like a pirate upon the gallows or gibbet, for speaking a *word* or making a *sign* merely, let them go to the south, and proclaim their opposition to " slavery in the abstract," in the ears of those who enforce the laws above noticed; then we will believe them.

10. *Higher than the highest.*

We cannot be reminded too often of this solemn truth; — God is infinitely acquainted with everything that in any way concerns the oppressor and the oppressed; and He is pledged to deliver all such as are afflicted, when they call upon him in faith.

11. *Maketh wise men mad.*

The word here rendered *mad* is from *halal*, which signifies, among other things, *to be haughty, arrogant, wicked.* If *mad* be the correct rendering of it, here, we might inquire, whether *oppression* produces this effect upon the enslaver, or the enslaved, or whether this effect be produced upon both as well as upon those who look on and witness its effects, in others. Admitting those are *mad* who are praying for the abolition of slavery, as some pretend to believe, this state of mind is produced, it must be remembered, by the *crimes* of others, and perhaps it were as desirable to suffer it, as it is to be

" Frighted when a madman stares."

But it is, however, a well known fact, that one of the first and most direct influences which the slave-system produces upon the minds of all who become connected with it, is to render their dispositions *arrogant* and *haughty*. The following testimony from Thomas Jefferson may be considered as conclusive evidence upon this point.

"The whole commerce between master and slave, is a perpetual exercise of the most boisterous passions, the most unremitting despotism on one part, and degrading submissions on the other. The parent storms, the child looks on, catches the lineaments of wrath, puts on the same airs in the circle of smaller slaves, gives a loose to his *worst of passions;* and thus nursed, educated, and daily exercised in *tyranny*, cannot but be stamped by it with odious peculiarities. The man must be a prodigy who can retain his manners and morals undepraved by such circumstances."

CHAPTER VI.

ISAIAH.

God commands the oppressor most explicitly to let the oppressed go free.

1. Cease to do evil; learn to do well; seek judgment, relieve the oppressed; judge the fatherless; plead for the widow. Isa. 1: 16.
2. For the vineyard of the LORD of hosts is the house of Israel, and the men of Judah his pleasant plant; and he looked for judgment, but behold oppression; for righteousness, but behold a cry. Isa. 5: 7.
3. Therefore the LORD shall have no joy in their young men, neither shall have mercy on their fatherless and widows: for every one is an hypocrite and an evil doer, and every mouth speaketh folly. Isa. 9: 17.

4. And they shall take them captives whose captives they were, and they shall rule over their oppressors. And it shall come to pass in the day that the LORD shall give thee rest from thy sorrow, and from thy fear, and from the hard bondage wherein thou wast made to serve. Isa. 14: 2.

5. For they shall cry unto the LORD because of the oppressors, and he shall send them a Savior, and a great one, and he shall deliver them. Isa. 19: 20.

6. Wherefore thus saith the Holy One of Israel, Because ye despise this word, and trust in oppression and perverseness, and stay thereon; therefore this iniquity shall be to you as a breach ready to fall, swelling out in a high wall, whose breaking cometh suddenly at an instant. Isa. 30: 12.

7. He that despiseth the gain of oppressions, that shaketh his hands from holding of bribes, that stoppeth his ears from hearing of blood, and shutteth his eyes from seeing evil; he shall dwell on high; his place of defence shall be the munitions of rocks; bread shall be given him, his waters shall be sure. Isa. 33: 15.

8. I have raised him up in righteousness, and I will direct all his ways; he shall build my city, and he shall let go my captives; not for price nor reward, saith the LORD of hosts. Isa. 45: 13.

9. Thus saith thy Lord the LORD, and thy God that pleadeth the cause of his people, Behold I have taken out of thine hand the cup of trembling, even the dregs of the cup of my fury; — but I will put it into the hand of them that afflict thee; which have said to thy soul, bow down, that we may go over; and thou hast laid thy body as the ground,

and as the street to them that went over. Isa. 51: 22.

10. Cry aloud, spare not; lift up thy voice like a trumpet, and show my people their transgression, and the house of Jacob their sins. Isa. 58: 1.

11. Is not this the fast that I have chosen? to loose the bands of wickedness, to undo the heavy burdens, and to let the oppressed go free, and that ye break every yoke? Isa. 58: 6.

12. Is it not to deal thy bread to the hungry, and that thou bring the poor that are cast out to thy house? when thou seest the naked that thou cover him; and that thou hide not thyself from thine own flesh? Isa. 58: 7.

13. Then shall thy light break forth as the morning, and thine health shall spring forth speedily; and thy righteousness shall go before thee, the glory of the Lord shall be thy rereward. Isa. 58: 8.

14. Then shalt thou call, and the Lord shall answer; thou shall cry, and he shall say, Here I am. If thou take away from the midst of thee the yoke, the putting forth of the finger, and speaking vanity. Isa. 58: 9.

15. And if thou draw out thy soul to the hungry, and satisfy the afflicted soul; then shall thy light rise in obscurity, and thy darkness be as the noonday. Isa. 58: 10.

16. And the Lord shall guide thee continually, and satisfy thy soul in drought, and make fat thy bones; and thou shalt be like a watered garden, and like a spring of water, whose waters fail not. Isa. 58: 11.

17. And they that shall be of thee shall build

the old waste places ; thou shalt raise up the foundations of many generations ; and thou shalt be called, the Repairer of the breach, the Restorer of paths to dwell in. Isa. 58 : 12.

18. For your hands are defiled with blood, and your fingers with iniquity ; your lips have spoken lies, your tongue hath muttered perverseness. Isa. 59 : 3.

19. Their feet run to evil, and they make haste to shed innocent blood ; their thoughts are thoughts of iniquity, wasting and destruction are in their paths. The way of peace they know not ; and there is no judgment in their goings, they have made them crooked paths ; whosoever goeth therein shall not know peace. Isa. 59 : 7.

20. Therefore is judgment far from us, neither doth justice overtake us ; we wait for light but behold obscurity ; for brightness, but we walk in darkness. Isa. 59 : 9.

21. For our transgressions are multiplied before thee, and our sins testify against us ; — in transgressing and lying against the Lord, and departing away from our God, speaking oppression and revolt, conceiving and uttering from the heart words of falsehood. 59 : 12.

22. And judgment is turned away backward, and justice standeth afar off ; for truth is fallen in the street, and equity cannot enter. Yea, truth faileth ; and he that departeth from evil maketh himself a prey ; and the Lord saw it, and it displeased him, that there was no judgment. Isa. 59 : 14.

23. Cast ye up, cast ye up, prepare the way, take up the stumbling-block out of the way of my people. Isa. 57 : 14.

NOTES ON CHAPTER VI.

1. *Cease to do evil.*

And when this simple command of God is obeyed, slavery in all its forms will have been banished from the earth. The right of property in the souls and bodies of the human species, will have ceased forever. But, alas! how many frightful bug-bears have been conjured up in the imaginations of men against an immediate compliance with this command of God! To substitute, for the present authority of the "slave-master," a system of legal restraint, which should be adequately and impartially administered upon the slave population of this land, and to maintain such a system of laws by police regulations, as severe as the case might require, would, in the opinions of not a few, dissolve the unity of this nation! To abolish tyranny immediately, and establish law to supersede the right of the private master to use the club, and the cow-hide, — to make a magistrate, instead of the irresponsible master, the judge of what constitutes an offence, and to let an impartially chosen jury, judge, whether such offence has been committed, would, in the *fears* of many, be the greatest curse which could come upon the nation! And yet, this is all that is meant by *immediate abolition.*

3. *An hypocrite.*

Such, many, if not most of the persons who do not profess the Christian name, believe the generality of slave-holding Christians to be; and that there is a manifest and glaring inconsistency in the conduct of those Christians and Christian ministers who give their support to the slave-system, all persons know, who have reflected at all upon the subject.

4. *Take them captives whose captives they were.*

This was fulfilled in the restoration of the Jews from their state of captivity, when they took their enemies captives who had held them in bondage. So God has often caused the scales to turn in favor of the oppressed. The principles by which he governs the world are immutably the same; he *may* do this again.

6. *Because ye despise this word and trust in oppression.*

And is it not true to the very letter of this passage, that the enslavers both at the North and the South, in this land, do despise every effort which has been made to rid the country of slavery Do they not trust in oppression, and appeal to the laws by which they oppress the slaves, to prove their "rights," and to show how secure they are in the enjoyment of them? And if we may believe the truth set forth in this text, can we suppose that such are exposed to no danger, while in such a course of conduct?

8. *And he shall let go my captives, not for price nor reward.*

This evidently refers to Cyrus, the Persian king, whom God made a special agent for the liberation of the Jews from their Babylonian captivity. When he had captured the city, he let the Jews go free, without any *price* or *reward;* but certainly there would have been a thousand times more *justice* in his demanding a *price* for their liberation, than there is in the demand which the enslavers of this country make, for the freedom of those who have been laboring for their good ever since they were born. If justice in the latter case were to be done, the slaves would not only have their freedom restored to them of which they have been so *unjustly* deprived, but they would also receive a *large price*, not as a *gift*, indeed, but as a *just debt* for their long and arduous labors, and for the wrongs and sufferings which they have endured.

10. *Spare not.*

It is certainly painful to any sincere Christian, to feel himself under the necessity of reproving another for sin; but it is, nevertheless, a necessity which every faithful Christian will bear rather than sin himself against God and the souls of his fellow men. It is God who has said,— *Thou shalt in any wise rebuke thy neighbor, and not suffer sin upon him;* or as the margin reads, *that thou bear not sin for him.* Lev. 19: 17. He that sees his brother sin, and neglects through fear, or a false view of things, to reprove him, in a suitable way for it, becomes, thereby, in a measure, responsible for the sin of his neighbor, and he sins himself moreover in disobeying the above command of God.

11. *Let the oppressed go free.*

On this passage, the learned and pious Dr. A. Clarke, makes the following remarks:— "How can any nation pretend to fast or to worship God at all, or dare to profess that they believe in the existence of such a Being, while they carry on what is called the *slave-trade;* and traffic in the souls, blood, and bodies of men!

O ye most *flagitious* of KNAVES, and *worst* of HYPOCRITES, cast off at once, the *mask* of religion; and deepen not your endless perdition by professing the faith of our Lord Jesus Christ, while ye continue in this traffic!"

The trade here spoken of, is carried on now, as it has been for years past in this country, and thousands on thousands of men, women and children are every year bought and sold in this Christian land!

16. *The Lord shall guide thee continually.*

Let the reader observe, how many heavenly and most encouraging promises are held out in this and the four preceding verses, to such as comply with God's command concerning such as they now hold in bondage! What a pity that any Christian should lack faith to yield a ready obedience to God's word, and claim their present fulfillment!

17. *The old waste places.*

That there are such places in the slave-states, places which are made *waste* by the slave-system, the following extract will prove. It is from a speech delivered in the house of Virginia delegates, Jan. 14, 1832, by Thomas Marshall, Esq.

"Wherefore then object to slavery? Because it is *ruinous* to the whites — retards improvement — roots out an industrious population — banishes the yeomanry of the country — deprives the spinner, the weaver, the smith, the carpenter of employment and support. The evil admits of NO REMEDY. It is increasing, and will continue to increase until the whole country will be inundated with one black wave, covering its whole extent, with here and there a few white faces floating on its surface. The master has no capital but what is vested in human flesh; the father, instead of being richer for his sons, is at a loss to provide for them. There is no diversity of occupations, no incentives to enterprise. Labor of every species is disreputable because performed mostly by slaves. Our towns are *stationary*, our villages almost everywhere *declining ;* and the general aspect of the country, marks the curse of a *wasteful, idle, reckless population.* who have no interest in the soil, and care not how much it is impoverished. Public improvements are neglected; and the entire continent does not present a region for which nature has done so much and art so little."

18. *Your hands are defiled with blood.*

How true to the very letter, this and some of the following verses, describe the conduct of many in these United States, the following testimonies will show; they are from scores of the kind which might be adduced.

"The Winchester (Va.) Republican has an interesting narrative of a case of *kidnapping*, in which a woman was rescued, though the wretch who sold her to a trader in human flesh escaped. Dealing in slaves has become a *large business.* Establishments are made at several places in Maryland and Virginia, at which they are sold like cattle. These places of deposit are strongly built, and well supplied with *iron thumb-screws* and *gags*, and ornamented with *cow-skins* and other whips, oftentimes BLOODY. But the laws of these States permit the traffic, and it is suffered." — *Nile's Weekly Register for* 1829.

" To enumerate all the horrid and aggravating instances of men-stealing, which are known to have occurred in the State of Deleware, within the recollection of many of the citizens of that state, would require a volume. In many cases, *whole families* of free colored people, have been attacked in the night, beaten nearly to death with clubs, *gagged* and bound, and dragged into distant and hopeless slavery, leaving no traces behind except the BLOOD from their *wounds.*

" The ingenuity and stratagems employed by kidnappers, in effecting their designs, are such as to prove that the most consummate cunning is no evidence of wisdom or moral purity, nor incompatible with the most consummate villany. A monster in human shape, was detected in Philadelphia, pursuing the occupation of courting and marrying mulatto women, and selling them as slaves.

" From the best information that I have had opportunities to collect, I am fully convinced, that there are at this time, within the jurisdiction of the United States, *several thousands of legally free people of color, toiling under the yoke of involuntary servitude,* and transmitting the same fate to their posterity." — *Portraiture of Dom. Slav. &c. by Dr. J. Torry.*

22. *Maketh himself a prey.*

It is so common for men generally to practice iniquity, that he who repents and forsakes it, becomes a prey, a bye-word, and a reproach among his neighbors. The Rev. J. D. Paxton, formerly minister of a congregation at Cumberland Va., in right of his wife, was a slave-holder. But having with his pious companion, become convinced of the sin of enslaving the human species, he repented of his error and set his slaves free. He very soon after become a prey to the ill-will of those whose sins his conduct reproved, and was accordingly reproached and dismissed from his people.

A writer in the Christian Advocate and Journal, a religious paper published at New York, stated, not long since, that the Rev. Dr. Coke, one of the first bishops of the Methodist Episcopal church, said and preached so much against the sin of slavery, at the South, that it was thirty years before the enslavers whom it irritated, ceased to reproach the Dr., and the people with whom he was connected, on this account! This was said to show the *impolicy* of preaching against slavery, at the present day!

CHAPTER VII.

JEREMIAH.

God has pronounced the bitterest of woes upon all such as are concerned in stealing men, — and upon all such as use the labors of their species without wages.

1. For among my people are found wicked men; they lay wait, as he that setteth snares; they set a trap, they catch men. Jer. 5 : 26.
2. They are waxen fat, they shine; yea they overpass the deeds of the wicked; they judge not the cause, the cause of the fatherless, yet they

prosper; and the right of the needy do they not judge. Jer. 5: 28.

3. For if ye throughly amend your ways and your doings; if ye throughly execute judgment between a man and his neighbor; if ye oppress not the stranger, the fatherless and the widow, and shed not innocent blood in this place; then will I cause you to dwell in this place, in the land that I gave to your fathers, forever and ever. Jer. 7: 5.

4. Oh that my head were waters, and mine eyes a fountain of tears, that I might weep day and night for the slain of the daughter of my people. Oh that I might leave my people and go from them! for they be all adulterers, an assembly of treacherous men. Jer. 9: 1.

5. Thus saith the LORD, Execute judgment in the morning, and deliver him that is spoiled out of the hand of the oppressor, lest my fury go out like fire, and burn that none can quench it, because of the evil of your doings. Jer. 21: 12.

6. Thus saith the LORD, Execute ye judgment and righteousness, and deliver the spoiled out of the hand of the oppressor; and do no wrong, do no violence to the stranger, the fatherless nor the widow, neither shed innocent blood in this place. Jer. 22: 3.

7. Woe unto him that buildeth his house by unrighteousness, and his chambers by wrong; that useth his neighbor's service without wages, and giveth him not for his work. Jer. 22: 13.

8. But thine eyes and thine heart are not but for thy covetousness, and for to shed innocent blood, and for oppression, and for violence to do it. Jer. 22: 17.

9. And ye shall seek me, and find me, when ye

shall search for me with all your heart. And I will be found of you saith the Lord; and I will turn away your captivity, and I will gather you from all the nations, and from all the places whither I have driven you, saith the Lord. Jer. 29 : 13.

10. Now when all the princes and all the people which had entered into the covenant, heard that every one should let his man-servant, and every one his maid-servant go free, that none should serve themselves of them any more, then they obeyed and let them go. Jer. 34 : 10.

11. But afterward they turned, and caused the servants and the hand-maids, whom they had let go free, to return, and brought them into subjection for servants and for hand-maids. Jer. 34 : 11.

12. Therefore thus saith the Lord; ye have not hearkened unto me, in proclaiming liberty, every one to his brother, and every man to his neighbor; behold I proclaim a liberty for you, saith the Lord, to the sword, to the pestilence, and to the famine. Jer. 34 : 17.

13. Thus saith the Lord of hosts, The children of Israel and the children of Judah were oppressed together; and all that took them captives held them fast; they refused to let them go. Their Redeemer is strong; the Lord of hosts is his name; he shall throughly plead their cause, that he may give rest to the land. Jer. 50 : 33, 34.

NOTES ON CHAPTER VII.

1. *They set a trap; they catch men.*

The Rev. G. Bourne, who resided some time in Virginia, remarks concerning the "*man catchers*" and their "*traps*" in this country as follows:—

"Nothing is more common than for two of these white partners in iniquity, Satan-like, to start upon the prowl, and if they find a free man upon the road, to demand his certificate, [a certain writing which all free colored people at the South must have with them, or be deemed and taken for slaves] tear it in pieces or secrete it, tie him to one of their horses, hurry to some jail, while one whips the citizen along as fast as their horses can travel. There, by an understanding with the jailor, who SHARES in the spoil, all possibility of intercourse with his friends is cut off. At the earliest possible period, the captive is sold to pay the felonious claims of the law, brought through jugglery by this trio of man-stealers; and then transferred to some of their accomplices in iniquity, who fill every part of the Southern states with fraud, rapine, and blood."

Dr. Torry, before mentioned, describes another kind of " trap " by which thousands of poor souls have been " caught " in this land of Christians; he says; — " They have lately [this was in 1817] invented a method of attaining their objects through the instrumentality of the laws. Having selected a suitable free colored person, to make a pitch upon, the conjuring kidnapper employs a confederate, to ascertain the distinguishing marks of his body, and then claims and obtains him as a slave, before a magistrate, by describing those marks, and proving the truth of his assertions by his well instructed accomplice."

And here is another; it is given by a member of the Lane Seminary, and it may be relied upon as a correct representation of scores of similar " traps " which are set in many other parts of the nation. He says: —

" A member of this institution, recently visiting among the colored people of Cincinnati, entered a house where was a mother and her little son. The wretched appearance of the house induced the visitor to suppose that the husband of the woman must be a drunkard. He inquired of the boy, who was about two or three years old, where his father was? He replied, '*Papa stole.*' The visitor seemed not to understand, and, turning to the mother, said, ' what does he mean?' She then related the following circumstances. About two years ago, one evening her husband was sitting in the house, when two men came in, and professing great friendship, persuaded him, under some pretence, to go on board a steamboat, then lying at the dock, and bound down the river. After some hesitation he consented to go. She heard nothing from him after this, for more than a year, but supposed he had been kidnapped. In the spring of 1833, Dr. —— of Cincinnati, saw him and recognized him, in a drove of slaves, at Natchez, Miss. and in a conversation which he held with him, he learned, that the negro, had been driven about from place to place, since he was decoyed from home, by the 'soul-drivers,' had been bought and sold two or three times, and once he had been immured within the walls of a jail for safe keeping." And see the 18th note in the preceding chapter, where other kinds of "man-traps" are described, and by which, the free and unoffending citizens of this Republic are *caught* and *enslaved*.

4. *They be all adulterers.*

And in view of the crimes of this nature, which, are fostered, legalized, and perpetuated by the slave-system, with what propriety may one adopt the language of this text! Take the following as evidence upon this point; in reading these facts, the reader will see, perhaps, the reasons, why we are so often desired by the pro-slavery party not to touch this " delicate subject."

"There is one feature of this nefarious traffic [the Domestic Slave Trade] which no motives of delicacy, can induce me to omit mentioning. Shall we conceal the truth, because its revelation will shock the finer sensibilities of the soul, when by such concealment we shut out all hope of remedying an evil, which dooms to a dishonored life, and to a hopeless death, thousands of the females of our country? Is this wise? Is it prudent? Is it *right*? I allude to the fact, that large numbers of female mulattoes are annually brought up, and carried down to our southern cities, and sold at enormous prices for purposes of private prostitution. This is a fact of universal notoriety in the south-western states. It is known to every soul-driver in the nation. And is it so *bad* that Christians may not know it, and, knowing it, apply the remedy? In the consummation of this nameless abomination, threats and the lash come in, where kind promises, and money fail. And will not the mothers of America feel in view of these facts?" *H. B. Stanton.*

" The law does not recognize marriages among slaves, so as to clothe them with the rights and immunities, which are given to this state, among citizens. The owner of either party may, the next day, or hour, break up the connection in any way he pleases. In fact, these connections have no protection, and are so often broken up by sales and transfers and removals, that they are by the slaves often called 'taking up together.' The sense of marriage fidelity must be greatly weakened, if not wholly destroyed by such a state of things. The effect is most disastrous.

"But there are other circumstances which deserve our notice. What effect is likely to be produced on the morals of the whites, from having about them, and under their absolute authority, female slaves, who are deprived of the strongest motives to purity, and exposed to peculiar temptations to opposite conduct! The condition of female slaves is such, that promises and threatenings and management can hardly fail to conquer them. They are entirely dependent on their master. They have no way to make a shilling to procure any article they need. Like all poor people, they are fond of finery, and wish to imitate those who are above them. What, now, are not presents and kind treatment, likely to effect on such persons? And the fact, that their children, should they have any through such intercourse, may expect better treatment from so near relations, may have its influence. That the vice prevails to a most shameful extent, is proved from the rapid increase of mulattoes. Oh, how many have fallen before this temptation; so many, that it has almost ceased to be a shame to fall! Oh, how many parents may trace the impiety and licentiousness and shame of their prodigal sons, to the temptations found in the female slaves of their own or their neighbors' households! And many a lovely and excellent woman, confiding in vows of affection and fidelity, trusting to her power over her devoted lover, has, after uniting her fate with his, and giving him all that a woman has to give, found, when too late, how incorrigible are those habits of roving desire, formed in youth, and kept alive by the temptations and facilities of the slave system.

"Now, when we read the repeated declarations that '*fornicators and adulterers shalt not inherit the kingdom of God*,' and call to mind the teachings of our Lord, that all intercourse between the sexes, except what takes place between one man and one woman in marriage faith, amounts to those crimes; how can we, as believers in Christianity, uphold a system which presents this temptation both to the bond and free, and yet escape a participation in the guilt?" *Rev. J. D. Paxton.*

"Again, slaves, in consequence of the manner in which they are raised, are generally prone to vicious indulgences, and many of them are exceedingly profligate: their master's children often mingle with them, and not only witness their vicious practices, but also listen to their lascivious conversation, and thus from infancy they become familiar with almost everything wicked and obscene, And this, in connection with easy access, becomes a strong temptation to lewdness. Hence it often happens, that the master's children practice the same vices which prevail among his slaves; and even the master himself is liable to be overwhelmed by the floods of temptation. And in some instances the father and his sons are involved in one common ruin; nor do the daughters always escape this impetuous fountain of pollution. Were it necessary, I could refer you to several instances of slaves actually seducing the daughters of their masters! Such seductions sometimes happen, even in the most respectable slave-holding families." *Rev. John Rankin.*

Other testimonies of a similar kind, and from the most credible persons residing in the slave states, might be given, were it necessary. Perhaps the reader is aware, how often we have been told, by the pro-slavery party, that, to abolish the slave system, would lead to an amalgamation of the whites and blacks of this country! The persons, who make the above objection, however, against the anti-slavery movements of the present day, do not seem to feel any great repugnance against the "amalgamation" described in the above extracts, which now prevails to such an alarming and disgraceful extent, at the south and west.

7. *Woe unto him, that useth his neighbor's services without wages.*

And how could there be a more faithful description of the slave-holding which prevails in this country, than is found in this passage of Scripture? Nor does it invalidate this remark; to say that the prophet did not have this system in his mind when he uttered these words; who *knows* that he did not? The truth is, there is not one sin of any kind, committed at the present day, which is more directly and explicitly described in the language of the Bible, than the *sin* of *slave-holding*, is in this text;—not one! Who *builds his house by wrong*, by the fruits of another's labor? *The enslaver of the human species. Who uses his neighbor's services without giving him wages* in return? Who compels his *neighbor* to toil from day to day, and from year to year, without *giving him wages for his work? The* SLAVE-HOLDER! And, reader, what does the infinite God, say concerning such, in this text?

CHAPTER VIII.

EZEKIEL — DANIEL — HOSEA — JOEL — AMOS — JONAH — MICAH — NAHUM — HABAKKUK — ZECHARIAH — AND MALACHI.

Various features of the slave-system, most aptly described in the language of the Bible.

1. Thus saith the LORD God, woe to the women that sew pillows to all arm-holes, and make kerchiefs upon the head of every stature to hunt souls! Will ye hunt the souls of my people, — and will ye pollute me among my people, for handfuls of barley and for pieces of bread, to slay the souls that should not die, and to save the souls alive, that should not live, by your lying to my people, that hear your lies? Ezek. 13 : 18.

2. If a man be just — and hath not oppressed any, but hath restored to the debtor his pledge, hath spoiled none by violence, hath given his bread to the hungry, and hath covered the naked with a garment; — hath executed true judgment between man and man, he shall surely live, saith the LORD God. Ezek. 18 : 5 — 9.

3. Her princes in the midst thereof are like wolves ravening the prey, to shed blood, and to destroy souls, to get dishonest gain. Ezek. 22 : 27.

4. And her prophets have daubed them with untempered mortar, seeing vanity, and divining lies unto them, saying, Thus saith the LORD God, when the LORD hath not spoken. Ezek. 22 : 28.

5. The people of the land have used oppression, and exercised robbery, and have vexed the poor and needy; yea, they have oppressed the stranger wrongfully. Ezek. 22: 29.

6. They traded the persons of men, and vessels of brass in thy market. Ezek. 27: 13.

7. Break off thy sins by righteousness, and thine iniquities by showing mercy to the poor. Dan. 4: 27.

8. He is a merchant, the balances of deceit are in his hand, he loveth to oppress. Hos. 12: 7.

9. And they have cast lots for my people; and have given a boy for an harlot, and sold a girl for wine, that they might drink. Joel 3: 3.

10. The children also of Judah and the children of Jerusalem have ye sold unto the Grecians, that ye might remove them far from their border. Behold, I will raise them out of the place whither ye have sold them, and will return your recompense upon your own head. Joel 3: 6.

11. Thus saith the Lord, for three transgressions of Israel, and for four, I will not turn away the punishment thereof, because they sold the righteous for silver, and the poor for a pair of shoes; and a man and his father will go in unto the same maid, to profane my holy name. Amos 2: 6.

12. Let man and beast be covered with sackcloth, and cry mightily unto God; yea, let them turn every one from his evil way, and from the violence that is in their hands; who can tell if God will turn and repent, and turn away from his fierce anger, that we perish not? Jonah 3: 8.

13. He hath showed thee, O man, what is good; and what doth the Lord require of thee, but to do

justly, and to love mercy, and to walk humbly with thy God? Mic. 6: 8.

14. Woe to the bloody city! it is all full of lies and robberies; the prey departeth not; the noise of a whip, — because of the multitude of the whoredoms of the well-favored harlot, the mistress of witchcrafts, that selleth nations through her whoredoms, and families through her witchcrafts. Na. 3: 1 — 4.

15. Therefore the law is slacked, and judgment doth never go forth; for the wicked doth compass about the righteous; therefore wrong judgment proceedeth. Hab. 1: 4.

16. Thus saith the Lord my God; Feed the flock of the slaughter, whose possessors slay them, and hold themselves not guilty; and they that sell them say, Blessed be the Lord, for I am rich; and their own shepherds pity them not. Zec. 11: 4.

17. Have we not all one father? hath not one God created us? Why do we deal treacherously every man against his brother, by profaning the covenant of our fathers? Mal. 2: 10.

18. And I will come near to you, to judgment; and I will be a swift witness against the sorcerers, and against the adulterers, and against false swearers, and against those that oppress the hireling in his wages, the widow, and the fatherless, and that turn aside the stranger from his right, and fear not me, saith the Lord of hosts. Mal. 3: 5.

NOTES ON CHAPTER VIII.

1. *Will ye hunt the souls of my people?*

A negro hunt is a common occurrence in the slave-states. "When negroes run away from the happiness which their masters say they enjoy at home, a hunt is immediately set on foot. In the pursuit, with dogs and guns, there appears to be not the least hesitation in shooting the fugitives, or tearing them in pieces. I recollect an extract from a private letter written near Edenton, N. C. two or three years ago, (before the Southampton insurrection,) which, among other matters of no great moment, mentioned that they had had '*great negro shooting lately.*' I have heard of shooting negroes from trees with as little concern, and apparently with as keen a zest, as a northern sportsman drops a squirrel or a quail." *D. L. Child, Esq.*

"Occasionally, armed parties of whites go in pursuit of them, who make no secret of their determination to shoot down all that refuse to surrender — which they sometimes do. In one instance, a negro who was closely pursued, instead of heeding the order to surrender, waded into a shallow pond, beyond the reach of his pursuers; refusing still to yield, he was shot through the heart by one of the party. This occurred near Natchez, but no notice was taken of it by the civil authorities; but in this they were consistent, for the city patroles, or night watch, are allowed to do the same thing with impunity, though it is authorized by no law.

"Another mode of capturing run-aways, is by blood-hounds; this I hope is rarely done. An instance was related to me in Clairborne county, Miss. A runaway was heard about the house in the night. The hound was put upon his track, and in the morning was found watching the dead body of the negro. The dogs are trained to this service while young. A negro is directed to go into the woods, and secure himself upon a tree. When sufficient time has been allowed for doing this, the hound is put upon his track. The blacks, also, are compelled to worry the hounds, till they make them their implacable enemies; and it is common to meet with dogs, which will take no notice of whites, though entire strangers, but will suffer no black, besides the house servants to enter the yard. Captured slaves are confined in jail till claimed by their owners. If they are not claimed within the time prescribed by law, they are sold at public sale, and in the mean time are employed as scavengers, with a heavy ball and chain fastened to one of their ancles." *A. S. Record, for March,* 1835.

2. *Hath spoiled none by* **violence.**

How often are we told, that the slaves of this country are so ignorant and degraded, that they are incapable of taking care of themselves. But how came they thus ignorant and degraded? Has the great God created a race of human beings, and made them incapable of taking care of themselves? If not, who has *spoiled* these human intelligences of that capacity? Who prevents their instruction? Who takes the fruit of their labors? And will a system which spoils millions of men women and children in this way, regenerate itself and restore what it has so wickedly taken away? Or, will those who in any way uphold this system, be the persons to fit the slaves for their liberty? And how will they do this, while they countenance and uphold slavery?

3. *To shed blood and to destroy souls.*

It is stated in the preamble to some resolutions introduced by Mr. Miner to the House of Representatives, in 1829, that "Officers of the federal government have been employed, and derive emoluments from carrying on the Domestic Slave-Trade." Indeed, the *princes* of this land are at the head of the slave-system.

"Droves of slaves are purchased by members of Congress, and conducted by themselves in person or by proxy, to their quarters. An honorable senator has been seen, several hundred miles from Washington, conveying a LOT of slaves, purchased during his official attendance in that city, almost to the very doors of the huts intended for their residence."—*Letter of J. G. Birney, Esq.*

4. *Her prophets have daubed them.*

And whether those ministers of this land, who attempt to justify the system of slave-holding from the Scriptures, do not imitate the conduct of the prophets, mentioned in this text, let the reader judge. A SLAVE-HOLDING *preacher!* There is, certainly, something indescribably repulsive in the thought of joining these two employments together! And how would the idea strike the reader, to contemplate *Jesus Christ* as an *enslaver* of the human species? How would it sound in the ear of a Christian, at this age of the world, to speak of *St. Paul* as a "*soul-driver,*" or a "*slave-holder?*"

5. *The people of the land have used oppression.*

And what wonder is it, if the people become oppressors, when their rulers, and their ministers set them the example?

6. *Traded the persons of men.*

This was their sin; they made merchandize of the souls and bodies of men, the same as many do now!

9. *Cast lots for my people.*

How aptly this passage of Scripture describes a part of the slave-system in this land, the following extract will show. It is from the *Picture of Slavery in the United States*, by the Rev. Mr. Bourne, before referred to. In accounting for the very great number of mulattoes which may be found upon some of the plantations at the South, whom he saw, he says:—" According to my companion's account, [a gentleman with whom he was travelling in Virginia,] there was a regular system established, by which it was scarcely possible for a child to be born without having some approximation to white, beyond that of the darkest of its generations; and that, between the owner of the plantation and his boys, and the overseer and his son, and their other artificers, he presumed that soon he would not have one black person upon the plantation." So true it is, that every abomination which was ever practiced among men, is now fostered and perpetuated by the slave-system!

CHAPTER IX.

JESUS CHRIST.

Our blessed Savior did as really describe and condemn the sin of slave-holding, as he did the sin of any other practice, to which men are now addicted.

1. Blessed are the merciful, for they shall obtain mercy. Matt. 5: 7.
2. Blessed are ye when men shall revile you and persecute you, and say all manner of evil against you falsely, for my sake. Matt. 5: 11.

3. Whosoever, therefore, shall break one of these least commandments, and shall teach men so, he shall be called the least in the kingdom of heaven; but whosoever shall do and teach them, the same shall be called great in the kingdom of heaven. Matt. 5: 19.

4. Therefore, if thou bring thy gift to the altar, and there rememberest, that thy brother hath aught against thee, leave there thy gift before the altar, and go thy way; first be reconciled to thy brother, and then come and offer thy gift. Matt 5: 23.

5. Love your enemies, bless them that curse you, do good to them that hate you, and pray for them that despitefully use you, and persecute you. Matt. 5: 44.

6. Therefore, all things whatsoever ye would that men should do to you, do ye even so to them, for this is the law and the prophets. Matt. 7: 12.

7. Go ye and learn what that meaneth, I will have mercy and not sacrifice. Matt. 9: 13.

8. Jesus said unto him, Thou shalt love the Lord thy God with all thy heart, and with all thy soul, and with all thy mind. This is the first and great commandment. And the second is like unto it, Thou shalt love thy neighbor as thyself. Matt. 22: 37.

9. Woe unto you, scribes and Pharisees, hypocrites! for ye pay tithe of mint, and anise, and cummin, and have omitted the weightier matters of the law, judgment, mercy, and faith; these ought ye to have done, and not to leave the other undone. Matt. 23: 23.

10. Then shall they also answer him, saying, Lord, when saw we thee a hungered, or athirst, or a stranger, or naked, or sick, or in prison, and

did not minister unto thee? Then shall he answer them, saying, Verily, I say unto you, Inasmuch, as ye did it not to one of the least of these, ye did it not to me. Matt. 25 : 44.

11. The Spirit of the Lord is upon me, because he hath anointed me to preach the gospel to the poor; he hath sent me to heal the broken-hearted, to preach deliverance to the captives, and recovering of sight to the blind, to set at liberty them that are bruised, to preach the acceptable year of the Lord. Luke 4 : 18.

12. Be ye therefore merciful, as your Father also is merciful. Luke 6 : 36.

13. Take heed and beware of covetousness; for a man's life consisteth not in the abundance of the things which he possesseth. Luke 12 : 15.

14. These things I command you, that ye love one another. John 15 : 17. This is my commandment, that ye love one another, as I have loved you. John 15 : 12.

15. God anointed Jesus of Nazareth with the Holy Ghost and with power; who went about doing good, and healing all that were oppressed of the devil. Acts 10 : 38.

16. Which now of these three, thinkest thou, was neighbor unto him that fell among the thieves? And he said, He that showed mercy on him. Then said Jesus unto him, Go and do thou likewise. Luke 10 : 36.

NOTES ON CHAPTER IX.

1. *They shall obtain mercy.*

Mercy, from *misericordia;* and this from *miserans*, pitying, and *cor*, the heart, or *miseria cordi*, pain of heart. It signifies that pain which one feels upon the sight or knowledge of another who is in misery, and which leads him to the use of suitable means for his relief. How do the enslavers of the human species show mercy toward those whom they deprive of their liberty, and from whom they keep back the price of their labor? "How shalt thou hope for mercy, rendering none?"

2. *When men shall persecute you.*

And does the blessing here pronounced upon the persecuted, authorize another to persecute them? It certainly does, if those precepts which enjoin obedience upon servants, may be quoted as a justification of the conduct of the enslavers who deprive them of their liberty.

3. *Whosoever shall break one of these commandments.*

"What an awful consideration is this! He who by his mode of *acting*, *speaking*, or *explaining*, the word of God, sets the holy precept *aside*, or explains away its *force* and *meaning*, shall be called least, shall have no place in the kingdom of Christ here, nor in the kingdom of glory above."—*Dr. Clarke.*

Let those ministers and members of Christian churches who hold their species in bondage, reflect on these fearful words of unerring truth; and when they do this, let them remember, how much dependence is made upon their example, by other enslavers who do not profess to love God! And then let them ask themselves, whether they do not break *one of the least of God's commandments*, with regard to the poor and needy, and whether they do not, in some sense, teach others to do the same?

4. *First be reconciled to thy brother.*

And how can a professing Christian be reconciled to a brother, whom he violently holds in bonds? How can a believer in the truth of the Bible, help remembering, when he approaches the altar of God in prayer, that every one of his poor defenceless slaves *has* AUGHT *against him!* He withholds from them their liberty, the greatest of all earthly blessings; and have they *nothing* against him? He deprives them of the fruit of their labor; have they *nothing* against him? He deprives the parents of their right to their own offspring; have they *nothing* against him? He parts the wife from her husband, and the husband from his wife; have they *nothing* against him? He gives his example in support of a violent and most wicked and cruel system of bondage, a system which perpetuates the horrid traffic in human souls, in human flesh and blood; have they *nothing* against him? Has no slave in this land, *any* thing against such a Christian, when he thus gives his influence to support a system, which robs and grinds to the very dust more than two millions of men women and children? A system which shuts from their minds the lights of science and religion, a system which is made up of the worst kind of theft, and which defrauds the poor and friendless, destroys feminine modesty, and corrupts all classes in society where it prevails with every shade of vice and irreligion? In a word, if every poor slave in this nation, have not enough in the sight of God, against every Christian enslaver of the human species, to prevent their prayers from being heard, unless they repent, then are these words of God, utterly null and void, and without meaning to us.

5. *Love your enemies.*

This is one of the most sublime and heavenly precepts, which it was ever made the duty of men to obey; and by it men may justify themselves in becoming our enemies, in precisely the same way that others justify the system of slavery, by quoting those Scriptures which direct servants to obey their masters. And if we are to *love* those who are our enemies and who injure us, how much more should the master *love* his slaves, who have been his *friends*, and who have supported him in affluence and ease, ever since he was born?

6. *Do ye even so to them.*

And how could Christ have expressed himself more directly against slavery, than he has done in these words. Nor, indeed is it easy to conceive, that it could have been necessary for him to do so, even had it been possible. It is true, Christ might have described the *sin* of *slave-holding*, and condemned it by name; and so he could have described the sin of *polygamy*, and the sin of *rum drinking*, and the sin of *gambling*, with many other sins — but this he did not do; and shall we infer from this, that all these sins are allowed by the Son of God?

Now, does the enslaver of the human species do *as* he would be done by, in keeping his fellow men in bondage? And yet, how often must we be told, that "Christ never said anything against *slavery!*" *Nothing* against slavery! when he has laid down this rule for the conduct of all slave-holders; — ALL *things* WHATSO-

EVER *ye would that men should do to you,* DO *ye* EVEN SO *to them!*

But surely, nothing can be more evident than that there is just as much in this command against slavery as there is against theft, adultery, or murder.

7. *I will have mercy.*

These words are quoted from 1 Sam. 15: 22, and it would seem that many, even at this day, have to *learn what they mean.* The occasion upon which they were at first spoken, shows their meaning to be, that God prefers an act of mercy shown to his needy creatures, before any act of religious worship, to which one might be called at the same time. Indeed, the tenor of the whole Bible proves this; and yet, how many restrain their bowels of mercies towards the necessitous, and then go and worship God, to atone for their guilt in leaving undone their duty to the poor and needy. The following fact may be given as a faint illustration of the propriety and consistency of such a course of conduct.

A deacon in a certain town in New England, went to meeting one Sabbath, and left his hired man at home; on returning in the afternoon, from the house of God, he found that the man had not been at the church, as he anticipated, but had retired to some part of the farm. The deacon immediately commenced searching for him, and on proceeding to the place where they had been engaged the day before, in burning wood, he found the man seated upon a log near a fire which he had kindled. On the deacon's asking him how he came thus to absent himself from meeting, and to break the holy Sabbath, he replied as follows, — " Why, I only walked out here, and seeing the brands scattered around here and there, I just put them together, and then while they were burning, I thought I would sit down, and sing a *psalm tune* to take the fiery edge off."

8. *Thou shalt love thy neighbor as thyself.*

Do those professing Christians, do those ministers of the gospel, love their neighbors AS themselves, who have slaves in their families and upon their plantations, and the profits of whose labors they have been reaping for years, and who, at the same time, never have furnished these slaves with a Bible, nor suffered them to learn one single letter of the alphabet? Can they, do they, love their neighbors AS themselves, while they withhold from them their liberty, and take from them the fruit of their labor?

It may be said, we know, that the laws prohibit their teaching their slaves to read the Bible; but suppose the laws should forbid their praying for their slaves, or attempting their spiritual instruction in any way? Whom should we obey, God or man? The slave states have just as much *right* to prohibit, under the penalties of *fine, imprisonment* and DEATH, all kinds of prayer for the slaves, as they have to prohibit their instruction in letters, or in a Sabbath school; and every Christian might as consistently yield their support to such a law, as any do now, to those laws which prevent the slaves from being taught to read the word of God.

9. *And have omitted the weightier matters of the law.*

That law of God which requires *justice* between man and man, and *mercy* to the distressed; this law, if obeyed, would at once and forever annihilate slavery, from our nation and from the world. But alas! how many totally neglect this law, while, at the same time, they are exceedingly punctilious in *paying tithe of mint, and anise, and cummin;* nor do they seem to realize what a drawback the sin of slave-holding is, upon the virtues of some who might otherwise be what their professions would seem to signify.

10. *Ye did it not to one of the least of these my brethren.*

Hence, it is indisputable, that Christ considers the good or the evil which is done unto one of the least of his followers, as actually done unto himself. Now suppose for one moment, that slavery is not an evil; suppose it is consistent and right for a Christian to buy and sell men women and children, and hold them as his *property.* Is there any professing Christian, or any minister of the gospel who would deal thus with the person of Jesus Christ, were he now here upon earth? How does it seem to the reader, to think of JESUS CHRIST, set up at auction, *bought* and *sold, yoked with an iron collar, chained, scourged* and driven to work with a club or cowhide? But this is the kind of treatment which many of his *disciples* receive, and this too from those who claim to be their *Christian pastors,* and their brethren in the Lord! And these are they who tell us, — " Christ never said anything against slavery!"

11. *To preach deliverance to the captives.*

Though these words primarily refer to the spiritual deliverance which the gospel effects for sinners, who have been slaves to sin, yet, it is a fact, that the Christian religion does tend to promote the civil liberties of all nations where it is permitted to operate without restraint. Hence, in about three centuries after the birth of Christ, slavery was abolished throughout the Roman empire. Christianity has since abolished slavery in France, Spain, Portugal, Sweden, Denmark, Prussia, Austria, Germany, and throughout the dominions of Great Britian; and in a word, *America is the only civilized Christian nation where slavery is permitted to exist!* And yet, we are the people to reproach other nations for their *tyrannies*, and to boast of our freedom and our *republican* laws and institutions!!!

The acceptable year of the Lord.

That is, the year of jubilee; as the Jews believed, their year of jubilee was typical of the redemption which was to be accomplished by the Messiah; and to this usage among the Jews the last clause of this text undoubtedly refers.

13. *Beware of covetousness.*

Beware of an eager, inordinate desire of that which belongs to another. If that is not covetousness which leads one to take possession of the liberty of his innocent fellow creatures, and to use their services without paying them wages for their labor, what is it? And covetousness, the apostle informs us, is *idolatry.* Col. 3: 5.

14. *As I have loved you.*

And how can the system of slave-holding stand in the presence of these words? *This is my commandment, that ye love one another as I have loved you.* That is, you should love one another as really, and as sincerely, in your sphere, as I have loved you in mine. It is not doubted but that some slave-holders may covet the liberty and labor of the slaves enough to risk their lives in the support of a system by which they can deprive them of these blessings, but does any enslaver love his slaves enough to lay down his life for them? Nay, does he love them enough to restore to them those blessings and rights of which he has so unjustly deprived them? Let the following fact speak on this subject; it was narrated by the Rev. M. B. Cox, late Missionary to Liberia, in one of the public papers, soon after the event occurred.

After the insurrection in Southampton, Va. which took place a few years ago, a slave-holder went into the woods in quest of some of the insurgents, accompanied by a faithful slave, who had been the means of saving his life in the time of the massacre. After they had been some time in the woods, the slave handed his musket to his master, informing him at the same time, that he could not live a *slave* any longer, and requesting him either to shoot him upon the spot, or set him free. The master took the gun from the hands of the slave, levelled it at his breast, and shot the faithful negro through the heart. Thus he was rewarded for his kindness to his master.

15. *Healing all that were oppressed of the devil.*

So, it seems, the devil himself is an *oppressor*, sinners are his slaves, and if we may credit the testimony of the Bible on this point, as well as the confessions of many of his faithful servants, he is a most rigorous and unfeeling *soul-driver*.

Speaking on the subject of slavery, the learned and pious Dr. A. Clarke, has expressed himself thus: — " I here register my testimony against the unprincipled, inhuman, anti-christian, and diabolical *slave-trade*, with all its *authors*, PROMOTERS, ABETTORS, and *sacriligious gains*, as well as against the great devil, the father of it, and them."

Here the devil is put down as the great father of all slave-holders, slave-dealers, and of all who defend and support the slave-system, in any way; and similar language might be quoted from almost every commentator, and Christian writer of any note which has ever lived. Take a few specimens: —

" *To slave-traders, and slave-holders.* You induce the villian to steal, rob, murder men, women and children, without number, by paying him for his execrable labor. It is all your act and deed. This equally concerns *all slave-holders, of whatever rank or degree;* seeing men-buyers are exactly on a level with men stealers! Indeed you say, ' I pay honestly for my goods; and I am not concerned to know how they are come by.' Nay, but you are; otherwise you are partaker with a thief, and are not a jot honester than he. But you know they are not honestly come by; you know they are procured by means *nothing near so innocent as picking pockets, house-breaking, or robbery upon the highway.* You know they are procured by a *deliberate species of more complicated* VILLANY, *of* FRAUD, ROBBERY *and* MURDER, than was ever practiced by Mohammedans or Pagans. Perhaps you will say, — ' I do not buy any slaves; I only use those left me by my father. But is that enough to satisfy your conscience ? Had your father, have *you*, has any man living a right to use another as a slave? It cannot be, even setting revelation aside.

"*The blood of thy brother crieth against thee from the earth.* O whatever it costs, put a stop to its cry before it be too late; *instantly*, at any price, were it the half of your goods; deliver thyself from *blood-guiltiness*. *Thy hands, thy bed, thy furniture, thy house and thy lands, at present, are stained with* BLOOD." *Rev. J. Wesley.*

"Men-stealers are inserted among these daring criminals, against whom the law of God directed its curses. These kidnapped men to sell them for slaves; and this practice seems inseparable from the other iniquities and oppressions of slavery; nor can a slave-dealer keep free from this criminality, if '*the receiver be* AS BAD AS THE THIEF.'"—*Scott.*

The following is from a number of resolutions which were passed in 1830, on this subject, by the Wesleyan Methodist Conference of preachers in England: —

"That as a body of Christian ministers, they feel themselves called upon again to record their *solemn judgment*, that the *holding of human beings in a state of slavery, is in* DIRECT OPPOSITION *to all the principles of natural right, and to the benign spirit of the religion of Christ.*"

"That the Conference fully concur in those *strong moral views of the* EVIL *of slavery*, which are taken by their fellow Christians of different denominations; — and that they express their sympathy with an injured portion of their race, and their ABHORRENCE *of all those principles* on which it is attempted to defend the subjection of human beings to hopeless and interminable slavery."

And quotations like the foregoing, might be added to the above, almost without number, but these are sufficient surely, to show the reader, that the Testimony of God is supported by the convictions and the judgment of the wisest and best of men, in denouncing *slave-holding* as a *sin*, and "a sin," as one of the commentators, above named, has remarked, "for which perdition itself, has scarcely an adequate state of punishment."

CHAPTER X.

ST. PAUL.

The Apostle Paul condemns slavery most explicitly — and shows that slave-holding is directly opposed to the spirit and temper of the Christian Religion.

1. Let love be without dissimulation. Abhor that which is evil; cleave to that which is good. Be kindly affectioned one to another, with brotherly love; in honor preferring one another. Rom. 12: 9.

2. Art thou called being a servant? care not for it; but if thou mayest be made free, use it rather. For he that is called in the Lord, being a servant, is the Lord's free man, likewise, also, he that is called, being free, is Christ's servant. 1 Cor. 7: 21.

3. Ye are bought with a price; be not ye the servants of men. 1 Cor. 7: 23.

4. Charity suffereth long and is kind; charity envieth not; charity vaunteth not itself, is not puffed up, doth not behave itself unseemly, seeketh not her own, is not easily provoked; thinketh no evil. 1 Cor. 13: 4.

5. Charity — beareth all things, believeth all things, hopeth all things, endureth all things. 1 Cor. 13: 7.

6. For, brethren, ye have been called unto liberty; only use not liberty for an occasion to the flesh, but by love serve one another. For all the

law is fulfilled in one word, even in this, Thou shalt love thy neighbor as thyself. Gal. 5: 13.

7. I therefore, the prisoner of the Lord, beseech you, that ye walk worthy of the vocation wherewith ye are called, with all lowliness and meekness, with long-suffering, forbearing one another in love. Eph. 4: 1.

8. And be ye kind one to another, tender-hearted, forgiving one another, even as God for Christ's sake hath forgiven you. Eph. 4: 32.

9. Servants be obedient to them that are your masters, according to the flesh, with fear and trembling, in singleness of your heart, as unto Christ. Knowing, that whatsoever good thing any man doeth, the same shall he receive of the Lord, whether he be bond or free. Eph. 6: 5.

10. And ye masters, do the same things unto them, forbearing threatening; knowing that your Master also is in heaven; neither is there respect of persons with him. Eph. 6: 9.

11. Let nothing be done through strife or vain glory; but in lowliness of mind let each esteem other better than themselves. Phil. 2: 3.

12. Finally, brethren, whatsoever things are true, whatsoever things are honest, whatsoever things are just; whatsoever things are pure, whatsoever things are lovely, whatsoever things are of good report; if there be any virtue, and if there be any praise, think on these things. Phil. 4: 8.

13. Masters, give unto your servants that which is just and equal; knowing that ye also have a Master in heaven. Col. 4: 1.

14. Withal praying also for us, that God would open unto us a door of utterance, to speak the mys-

tery of Christ, for which I am also in bond. Col. 4: 3.

15. And Paul said, I would to God, that not only thou, but also all that hear me this day, were both almost, and altogether such as I am, except these bonds. Acts 26: 29.

16. Put on therefore as the elect of God, holy and beloved, bowels of mercies, kindness, humbleness of mind, meekness, long-suffering, forbearing one another, and forgiving one another, if any man have a quarrel against any; even as Christ forgave you, so also do ye. Col. 3: 12.

17. Servants obey in all things your masters according to the flesh; not with eye service, as men pleasers, but in singleness of heart, fearing God. Col. 3: 22.

18. For this is the will of God — that no man go beyond and defraud his brother in any matter; because that the Lord is the avenger of all such, as we also have forewarned you and testified. 1 Thess. 4: 3.

19. Knowing this, that the law is not made for a righteous man, but for — the lawless, — for menstealers. 1 Tim. 1: 19.

20. Let as many servants as are under the yoke count their own masters worthy of all honor, that the name of God, and his doctrine be not blasphemed. And they that have believing masters, let them not despise them, because they are brethren; but rather do them service, because they are faithful and beloved, partakers of the benefit. 1 Tim. 6: 1.

21. Exhort servants to be obedient unto their own masters, and to please them well in all things;

not answering again; not purloining, but showing all good fidelity; that they may adorn the doctrine of God our Savior in all things. Tit. 2: 9.

22. Not now as a servant, but above a servant, a brother beloved, especially to me, but how much more unto thee, both in the flesh and in the Lord? If thou count me therefore a partner, receive him as myself. Phil. 16.

23. Remember them that are in bonds, as bound with them; and them which suffer adversity, as being yourselves also in the body. Heb. 13: 3.

NOTES ON CHAPTER X.

1. *Let love be without dissimulation.*

Let your tempers and actions correspond with your professions; you profess to love your neighbor as yourself;—act accordingly. But then, in examining these and similar passages, which bear so directly against slave-holding, we should remember, that it is not love, merely, which demands the immediate and total abolition of slavery in all its forms; for were love and kindness to be left entirely out of the question, the principles of equity and justice, if obeyed, would banish slavery from the church and from the world. But when the demands of justice are disregarded, then we may urge the principles of that *sincere* and *affectionate regard* which every Christian should feel towards his brother. And how can one who does really love God, and his neighbor, refuse obedience to the dictates of these principles as they are exhibited in this, and some of the following texts?

2. *Art thou a servant?*

The word here and elsewhere, (with but one exception) in the New Testament, rendered servant is $\delta o\tilde{v}\lambda o\varsigma$, and "it often implies," says Dr. A. Clarke, "*a servant* in general; or any one bound to the service of another, either for a *limited* time, or for life." But it is doubtful whether this term was ever used, either by Christ or any one of the Apostles, to signify one who was the entire and absolute property of another, as the slaves of this land are held, **for the following**, among other reasons:—

1. We know that Christ used this word to signify such as were not, and from the facts stated in the case, they could not have been the entire property of another. See Matt. 18: 23—35. Here we have an account of a δοῦλος, servant, who was so much in his master's debt, that he commanded him to be sold, and payment to be made, which would not have been done, had he been the absolute property of his master.

Slaves in Athens, who were held as the entire property of a master, were called οἰκέται, but *after* their FREEDOM was granted them, they were called δοῦλοι, not being like the former a part of the master's *estate*, but only required to render some small service such as was required of the μέτοεκοι, resident *strangers* or *aliens*, to whom in some respects, they were inferior. This the reader will learn by consulting Dr. W. Robinson's Antiquities of Greece, page 30 ; and Potter's Grecian Antiquities, Vol. I, page 18 ; and see also an article in the Bib. Repository, for Jan. 1835, " On slavery in Ancient Greece."

Now when we consider, that the Attic Greek is substantially the language in which the the New Testament was written, it seems the Apostles must have used the word δοῦλος, to signify a *freedman*, according to the authorities above quoted, and not one who was the entire property of another.

3. But it may be observed here, and once for all, that, if the Apostles used the word δοῦλος, to signify one who was the entire property of another, in the highest sense in which slaves were held as such among the Greeks and Romans, and if their directions to masters and their servants, are to be taken as a justification of the relation which the Roman and Grecian laws and customs established between such, then it must follow, that they justified everything which it authorized the master to do; for how could they justify the " relation " without justifying the parts of which it was composed? That relation authorized the master to do anything and everything to the person of his slave or " chattel " which he chose. He might scourge him, *maim* him, and even put him to *death* at his pleasure, and in doing these things he did not *abuse* this relation, but he exercised the civil rights which it conferred upon him. Nor indeed, was it the abuse of this relation which the Apostle forbid, when he

commanded the master to give unto his slaves, that which was just and equal, for, according to Dr. Taylor's "Elements of Civil Law," this relation among the Romans could not be abused in any way! Now it is allowed by all those who attempt to justify slavery from the Bible, that the apostles did positively forbid some things which this relation gave every master the right to do; and hence it follows as a consequence which cannot be denied, that the Apostles did positively forbid and condemn the relation which allowed them. How could the Apostles forbid *theft* without condemning at the same time the law which ALLOWS it? How could they condemn *murder* or *adultery*, without condemning at the same time the *law* which ALLOWS and JUSTIFIES these crimes.

4. But many persons of the present day imagine, that all the real objections which can now be brought against holding property in man, arise from the abuse of the relation which exists between the master and the enslaved, this, however, is a very great mistake. We do not argue against the abuse of this relation, nor indeed, do we found our arguments against it, upon the abuses of it, nor its liability to be abused; nay, it is the abuse of the relation, and its utter annihilation for which we contend. For this relation, it must be remembered, allows and justifies the master, in doing what the word of God forbids, and it not only allows of such things, but it makes it the master's duty to do them, and it imposes a penalty upon him, if he leaves them undone! This relation makes it the master's duty, to take the fruit of his neighbor's services — to crush his mind with ignorance, — to prevent him from obeying the command of God, which obligates all men to search the Holy Scriptures. Many other things this "relation" says the master may do, and these and many other wicked things it says the master *must* do, and in doing them he does not *abuse* the relation, but he FULFILLS it; and if he fulfills it, as the law makes it his duty to do, he does all in his power to oppress and crush the immortal mind of one of God's intelligent creatures, and so far as this relation is fulfilled and obeyed, its influence goes to send him down to the miseries of an eternal hell. Hence we say, that the relation is malum in se, so far as any relation can be which God has forbidden; and it seems not a little remarkable, that those who quote passages from the New Testament, to show that the Apostles justified this relation, seem never to have imagined that it belonged to them to show how the Apostles could

condemn the fruit of this relation, and yet not condemn the relation itself. And this every man should do before he attempts to justify this relation from anything which the Apostles have said, concerning any who may, possibly, have held it.

But even admitting that the δοῦλοι of whom the Apostles speak, in the following passages, were in some inferior sense held as the property of their masters, even this relation is condemned, as the reader will see.

2. *Care not for it.*

That is, do not let this hinder you from accepting of salvation at the hand of God. *But if thou mayest be made free, use it rather.* Use the first opportunity which may be offered to you for gaining your freedom.

3. *Be not ye the servants of men.*

Do not become slaves, if you can consistently prevent it. And what more need the Apostle have said, in order to *condemn slavery?* "Christians were at that time," as one writer on this subject has remarked, "when the Apostles wrote the epistles of the New Testament, under the government of the heathen; who were watching every opportunity to charge them with designs against the government, to justify their bloody persecutors. In such circumstances, had the Apostles proclaimed liberty to the slaves, many of them would have been exposed to certain destruction, and the Christian cause might have been ruined, without freeing a single slave; this would heve been the height of madness and cruelty." Hence the Apostles said everything which they could, consistently say, *at that time* to show the sin of slave-holding, and the right of the slave to his freedom. Nor did they say half so much to show the *sin of polygamy,* nor the *sin of theatres, lotteries, gambling* and many other practices which might be named.

4. *Seeketh not her own.*

The love of God leads all who possess it, to seek for the highest possible good of all with whom they have to do. "But," says one, "it is the highest possible good of the slave, that I should keep him in slavery, because, if I were to set him free, he would soon fall into the hands of another master, who might not treat him as well as I do," Now, admitting this to be true, in any given case, it would not, and could not follow from it, that the slave should not have his rights restored to him. That which might be the greatest possible

AGAINST SLAVERY. 87

good, to one individual slave, might, at the same time, be the greatest possible injury to the whole of the slave population as a class. And besides, does it follow, that because, another will rob my neighbor of his liberty and the fruit of his labor, that therefore, I ought to do it, because, I think I can do the work more *mildly* and *Christian-like* than he can? If, as it is sometimes thought, a Christian ought to hold his species in bondage, because if he does not do this, they will become slaves to another master, worse than he, then does it not follow, that Christians, ministers, legislators, and the very best men in the nation, should take the management of all the theatres and gambling houses in the country, into their hands? Should they not do all the murdering, thieving, and high-way robbery, in order to have it done *respectably Christian-like*, and in the *mildest* and *best manner* possible? If they do not do these things themselves, you know bad men will!

5. *Endureth all things.*

But many professing Christians do not possess enough of this heavenly virtue, to enable them to bear, the contumely which they *fear*, would be cast upon them, were they to do *justice* to those whom they have *wronged!*

6. *By love serve one another.*

You have been made free from the ceremonial law, and from sin by the gospel of Jesus Christ, and now it becomes your duty to serve one another, for in this way you are to fulfill the law of God. The Greek word, we have seen, which signifies a servant or *slave* is δοῦλος, and from this word we have the one in the text, which is rendered *serve;* δουλεύετε, *serve,* become *slaves,* in the performance of Christian duties, to one another. Hence it is the duty of every man professing the Christian name, in this sense, to become the slave of those whom he holds in bondage; this is the kind of slavery which is advocated in the Christian Scriptures; and accordingly, the Bible informs us, that Joshua was the slave of Moses, Elisha was the slave of Elijah, and St. Paul, St. Peter and the other Apostles were slaves of Jesus Christ, and Christ was the slave of God.

7. *Lowliness and meekness.*

How does the idea of *meekness* and *Christian humility* agree with that of a *soul-driver,* or *slave-holder?*

8. *Kind — tender-hearted.*

And many slave-holders, think they are so, because they are not so cruel and hard-hearted towards their slaves as some others. But how *very kind*, how *tender-hearted* one may be in comparison with another, when both of them *withhold* from you, your *personal* LIBERTY and *take from you the fruit of your labor*, it may not, indeed, be very easy to tell. However, that there are *slave-holders, soul-drivers*, and *dealers in* HUMAN SOULS, who may be called, *kind*, and *tender-hearted*, and *Christians*, when compared with others who might be named, no one will pretend to deny. O that they were *kind* and *tender-hearted* enough to restore to their poor slaves, the rights of which they have so unjustly *defrauded* them!

9. *Be obedient to them that are your masters.*

This is the language, which all abolitionists at the present day would use, were they permitted to have access to the slaves of this land. We could but enjoin it upon them to be patient and faithful. Our labor for their freedom is with God, and those who oppress them.

10. *Do the same things unto them.*

Here is the rule for the masters; and how soon their slaves would " go free," were it to be faithfully obeyed! No doubt, the slaves at the south, often hear their duties explained and enforced from the above, and some of the following passages in this chapter, but it is not so evident, that the duty of the master is as often enforced from this and similar texts.

11. *Better than themselves.*

The natural tendency of slavery upon the minds of the enslavers, is to lead them to think themselves better than others; thus the spirit of the gospel is reversed and counteracted. See the testimony of president Jefferson to this point, Chap. v. p. 49.

12. *Think on these things.*

For all of them are required by the gospel which you profess to love. But is there anything which is agreeable to the principles of unchangeable and eternal *truth* in slavery? Is there any *honesty* in it? any *purity*? anything *lovely* or of good report in the system, when " stripped of its abuses?" Then should we think of it, — we should *defend* it and *pray* for its continuance. Reader, perhaps you may have heard some one attempt to justify the system of slavery from the Bible, but did you ever hear any Christian or Christian minister *pray for its continuance and prosperity*?

And why not? If it is *right*, if it is *just*, if it is *consistent*, why not pray for it to prosper and continue as long as the world endures?

13. *That which is just and equal.*

We have before seen that, upon the supposition, that the masters to whom the Apostles gave this and similar directions, held their servants as their property " to all intents and purposes whatsoever," then it must follow, that this and similar commands must have been understood as a virtual condemnation of that " relation," which this right created between them; but no relation is condemned in these passages which does not allow the things which are here, and elsewhere forbidden; hence if the right of property in man were to cease this moment throughout this nation, there would be the same necessity for the commands and directions which are laid down in the New Testament for the instruction of servants and their masters; and if all masters do now obey this command of God towards their servants, they will pay them for their labor, and instruct them and prepare them as far as it is in their power to do it, for usefulness in the world. They will cease to hold them as *property*, and compel no one to work for them against his will. " But the laws will not suffer me to do this, — I must obey the laws." What! must you obey those laws which contravene the laws, of God! Did the prophet Daniel do so, when the government where he lived passed a law under a severe penalty, that he should not pray to the God of heaven?

Now when Daniel knew that the writing was signed, he went into his house; and his windows being open in his chamber toward Jerusalem, he kneeled upon his knees three times a day, and prayed, and gave thanks before his God, as he did aforetime, Dan. 6: 10. It is really too plain to need illustration, that if it would now be wrong for any of the enslavers to disobey the laws of the states where they live, which forbid them from instructing the slaves to read the word of God, and from paying them for their labor, then it was wrong for Daniel to pray to the God of heaven as he did, and it was also wrong for his companions to refuse to worship the golden image which the king had set up; and it was wrong also for the Apostles to " preach Christ and the resurrection," after they had been forbidden by the rulers, and scourged for so doing. See Acts 4: 19, and 5: 29.

15. *Except these bonds.*

It is not improbable that, when the Apostle uttered these words, he raised his hand or hands, so as to exhibit the chain with which he was bound; for the word here rendered *bonds*, signifies a *chain* or *fetters* with which a prisoner was confined. It seems that bondage was a *blessing*, which the venerable Apostle did not wish should descend upon others, not even his enemies! How many thousands of poor slaves in this land, many of whom are members of the Christian church, are compelled to wear the iron manacles, and when they pray to stretch out their *chained* hands unto God.

"The slaves which pass down to the southern market on the Mississippi river, and through the interior, — suffer great hardships. Those who are driven down by land, travel from two hundred to a thousand miles on foot. They sometimes carry *heavy chains* the whole distance. These chains are very massive. They extend from the hands to the feet, being fastened to the wrists and ancles by an iron ring round each. When chained, every slave carries two chains, that is, one from each hand to each foot." H. B. Stanton.

17. *Obey in all things your masters.*

It has been before remarked, that, if this and similar precepts, may be quoted to justify the power which the master usurps over his slaves, then the commands of Christ for the persecuted to pray for their persecutors, may be referred to, to justify persecution; and by the same rule of interpretation, we might show, that our forefathers sinned against God, in rebelling against the British government; and not only so, but, that the people of this country have been sinning ever since, in maintaining that independence which they asserted ! To such monstrous absurdities, those principles lead, which the enslavers adopt, in explaining the Scriptures so as to favor their system of oppression.

18. *Defraud his brother in any matter.*

One person may defraud another by corrupting his wife, or children; or by taking from him the fruit of his labor, or by withholding from him his personal liberty. To what lengths the poor slaves of this land have been defrauded, in all these respects, we must wait for the light of eternity to show.

19. *Men-stealers.*

But who are men-stealers? "Those *who carry on the traffic*

in human flesh and blood; those who *steal* a person in order to sell him into bondage; or those who buy such stolen men or women, no matter of what *color* or what country; or those who *sow dissensions* among barbarous tribes, in order that they who are taken in war may be sold into slavery. Or the *nations* who *legalize*, or *connive* at such traffic; all these are *men-stealers*, and God classes them with the most flagitious of mortals." *Dr. A. Clarke.*

" Stealers of men are all those who bring off slaves or freemen, and *keep, sell,* or *buy* them. To steal a freeman is the highest kind of theft. The word used here, in its original import, comprehends *all who are concerned in bringing any of the human race into slavery,* or in *detaining* them in it." *Presbyterian Conf. of Faith.*

" Man-stealers ! The worst of all thieves; in comparison of whom, high-way robbery and house-breakers are innocent;— and *men-buyers are exactly on a level with men-stealers.* That *execrable sum of all villanies,* commonly called the *slave-trade,* I read of nothing like it in the heathen world, whether ancient or modern, and it infinitely exceeds, in every instance of barbarity, whatever Christian slaves suffer in Mohammedan countries. — Liberty is the right of every human creature, as soon as he breathes the vital air, and no human law can deprive him of that right which he derives from the law of nature." *Rev. J. Wesley.*

" Men-stealers are inserted among these daring criminals (see 1 Tim. 1: 9, 10) against whom the law of God directed its awful curses. These kidnapped men to sell them for slaves; and this practice seems inseparable from the other iniquities and oppressions of slavery; nor can a *slave-dealer* keep free from this criminality if 'the receiver be as bad as the thief.' " *Scott.*

" A Christian buying and selling slaves ! A man, who professes that the leading law of his life, is to do as he would be done by, spending his time and amassing a fortune by buying and selling his fellow men." *Simpson.*

" They who make war, for the inhuman purpose of selling the vanquished as slaves, are really men-stealers. And they who *encourage* that *unchristian* traffic by purchasing the slaves which they know to be thus unjustly acquired are partakers in their crime." *Macknight.*

And the *intention* to enslave men, is put down as the same, or a similar *crime* by the Discipline of the Methodist Episcopal church. "*The buying and selling*, [this rule formerly read *The buying or selling*] *of men, women, and children, with an* INTENTION TO ENSLAVE *them.*" Dis. Ch. 2. Sec. 1.

It certainly cannot make material difference as to the manner of one's coming into the possession of men women and children, whether he *buys* them or receives them from another as a gift, or whether he takes possession of them by virtue of their birth, if it is his *intention to enslave* them, the Discipline of the M. E. church pronounces him an impenitent sinner.

20. *Worthy of all honor.*

Christianity does not alter the relation, which the laws of a land causes one man to sustain to another. If the laws are wrong, the only way by which even the Gospel can change them is, by rendering those wiser and better who make them; and by giving those grace and patience whom these laws injure and oppress. There is a difference between what the laws of a land require one to do, and that which they compel him to suffer; the former may be sinful, the latter not. It may be the duty of the slaves at the South to submit to the evils which the laws so unjustly inflict upon them, and in doing this, God has promised to reward them, if they do it with a view to his glory; while those who make and support these wicked laws by enslaving and oppressing their species, sin against God.

22. *Above a servant, a brother.*

And if all the slaves in this land were to run away from their masters, there is not a true abolitionist in the world, but who would consent for them to return again, on the conditions that they should be received and treated by their former masters, as Philemon is here commanded to receive Onesimus. It seems that Onesimus had been a servant to Philemon, and that for some cause which is not mentioned, he left his master, while in his debt. "If he hath wronged thee or oweth thee aught, put that to mine account." But having been converted to God under the labors of St. Paul, he directed him to return, and he wrote this Epistle in order to facilitate the adjustment of their difficulty. But Philemon was not now to be received as a slave, but *above a slave*, as a BROTHER BELOVED, even as the "aged Apostle" himself.

23. *Remember them that are in bonds.*

Those that are imprisoned for the testimony of Jesus, and all such as are kidnapped from their birth, and held during their whole lives in an unjust and violent bondage. Remember the rights, the privileges and the blessings of which they are deprived; remember it is the natural and direct tendency of the system which oppresses them to keep from their undying souls the lights of science and religion, to crush their immortal minds, and shut them out of heaven. Remember them, — feel for them, as you would wish others to feel for you, were you in their condition; pray for them, — pray for those who oppress them, — and pray for all those who *do not remember* them, but who censure and oppose those who endeavor to obey this command of the infinite God. REMEMBER THEM THAT ARE IN BONDS!

CHAPTER XI.

ST. JAMES, ST. PETER AND ST. JOHN.

Slave-holding is further shown to be a sin, by others of the Apostles — and we have the Testimony of God, that the system shall finally and utterly come to an end.

1. Do not rich men oppress you? — If ye fulfill the royal law, according to the Scripture, Thou shalt love thy neighbor as thyself, ye do well; but if ye have respect to persons, ye commit sin; and are convinced of the law as transgressors. James 2: 6.

2. For whosoever shall keep the whole law, and

yet offend in one point, he is guilty of all. James 2: 10.

3. For he shall have judgment without mercy, that hath showed no mercy, and mercy rejoiceth against judgment. James 2: 13.

4. But the wisdom that is from above is first pure, then peaceable, gentle, and easy to be entreated, full of mercy and good fruits, without partiality and without hypocrisy. James 3: 17.

5. Go to now, ye rich men, weep and howl for your miseries that shall come upon you. Your riches are corrupted, and your garments are moth eaten. Your gold and silver is cankered; and the rust of them shall be a witness against you, and shall eat your flesh as it were fire. James 5: 1.

6. Behold, the hire of the laborers who have reaped down your fields, which is of you kept back by fraud, crieth; and the cries of them which have reaped, are entered into the ears of the Lord of Sabaoth. James 5: 4.

7. Ye have lived in pleasure on the earth, and been wanton; ye have nourished your hearts as in a day of slaughter. Ye have condemned and killed the just; and he doth not resist you. James 5: 5.

8. And many shall follow their pernicious ways: by reason of whom the way of truth shall be evil spoken of. And through covetousness shall they with feigned words make merchandise of you; whose judgment now of a long time lingereth not, and their damnation slumbereth not. 2 Peter 2: 2.

9. Servants, be subject to your masters with all fear; not only to the good and the gentle, but also to the froward. For this is thankworthy, if a man

for conscience toward God, endure grief, suffering wrongfully. 1 Peter 2: 18.

10. Finally, be ye all of one mind, having compassion one of another; love as brethren, be pitiful, be courteous. 1 Peter 3: 8.

11. We know that we have passed from death unto life, because we love the brethren. He that loveth not his brother abideth in death. 1 John 3: 14.

12. Hereby perceive we the love of God, because he laid down his life for us; and we ought to lay down our lives for the brethren. 1 John 3: 16.

13. But whoso hath this world's good, and seeth his brother have need, and shutteth up his bowels of compassion from him, how dwelleth the love of God in him? 1 John 3: 17.

14. If a man say, I love God, and hateth his brother, he is a liar; for he that loveth not his brother whom he hath seen, how can he love God whom he hath not seen? 1 John 4: 20.

15. If there come any unto you, and bring not this doctrine, receive him not into your house, neither bid him God speed; for he that biddeth him God speed, is partaker of his evil deeds. 2 John 10.

16. And the merchants of the earth shall weep and mourn — for no man buyeth their merchandise any more; — the merchandize of — beasts, and sheep, and horses, and slaves, and souls of men. Rev. 18: 11 — 13.

NOTES ON CHAPTER XI.

1. *Do not rich men oppress you?*

And how exceedingly oppressed millions of our fellow citizens in this nation must necessarily be, in those states where their oath is not allowed in a court of JUSTICE, against a white man! Whether in a case of theft, rape, murder, or any other crime, the solemn testimony of a thousand persons with a colored skins, when against a white person, goes for nothing!

2. *He is guilty of all.*

He is as really guilty in the sight of God, who breaks *one* of his commands, as though he broke every one of them; though, he may not incur so much guilt. So we must conclude of persons who profess the Christian religion, and who at the same time indulge in habits which are contrary to the precepts and spirit of the gospel, such as making, vending, and using intoxicating liquors, visiting theatres, gambling in lotteries, and holding the human species in bondage; but which of these sins are the most heinous in the sight of God, is another question; but it is sufficiently evident, that each of them are transgressions of the Divine law, and he who commits either one of them, is as really guilty of resisting the authority of God, as if he committed them all.

3. *For he shall have judgment.*

The following fact, (which is but one of a thousand of the kind which might be given,) may serve to illustrate the first clause of this passage:—

"A master had repeatedly promised to manumit one of his slaves, who was an excellent black-smith, but he had as often violated his promise. The slave, elated with the hope of freedom, had worked earlier, later and harder, till at length, however, his heart grew sick, and *disappointment*, sharper than a serpents' tooth, relaxed the sinews of his arm, and poisoned his coarse and scanty fare. The master, to revive his spirits and restore his vigor, finally promised with unwonted solemnity, that if he would earn, by extra labor, a certain sum of money, amounting to several hundred dollars, he should be *free*. The slave fell to work once more, with redoubled energy. He toiled long and hard, and at last the blessed day dawned, on which, according to the stipulation of his master, he was to be enfranchised. But that treacherous and brutal individual, before the day arrived, had sold him to slave-trader to be carried away to New Orleans! and on that day he was destined to receive — not his promised pardon, but a new suit of *chains.*

"The heart-stricken man told his tale to the trader; — how he had been promised his freedom — how he had toiled, — what cherished and often deferred hopes would be blasted forever. He entreated him in the most touching language, to renounce the sacrilegious bargain, — but in vain. Finally, seeing that his prayers and tears were disregarded, he became desperate, and told the dealer, that if he did take him, one or the other of them must die, and that he then gave him fair warning. The trader was highly diverted, and said 'he liked such a spirited fellow.' He went on board a vessel, and, during a serene evening in that delicious climate, the trader reposed himself upon the deck. In the dead of the night, the slave contrived to rid himself of his hand-cuffs, and groped until he grasped a heavy hand-spike, and, thus armed, stood over the sleeping man. He waked him and told his purpose. 'Then God have mercy on me,' said the trader. 'God will not have mercy on you, neither will I' said the slave, and dashed out his brains."
D. L. Child, Esq.

5. *Shall eat your flesh as it were fire.*

What fearful language is here! Alas! for those who are so aptly described in the following verse, and to which these fearful denunciations, by the inspired writer, are applied.

6. *Kept back by fraud.*

Let the reader say whose fields are tilled and reaped by those to whom no wages are paid, in this land. See Chap. ii. 26, and vii. 5. If *slave-holding* is not set down as a SIN against God in this passage, and the others here referred to, then no sin is described in any part of the Bible.

8. *By reason of whom, &c.*

When persons err who profess the Christian religion, it gives the greatest occasion for the wicked and unbelieving to speak evil of Christianity. Hence it is, that the *example* of Christians who *make, vend,* and *use ardent spirit,* as an article of living or luxury, is so much deplored by all the true friends of the Temperance cause; and hence also, it is, that the *example* of Christians who *enslave* their *species,* tends, in so great a degree, to perpetuate the slavery system. As long as wicked and unprincipled men can refer to the *example* of *slave-holding ministers* and members of the Christian church, just so long slavery and the slave-trade will be continued.

9. *Be subject to your masters.*

See the note on Chap. x. 9. "Even a *slave*, if a Christian, was bound to serve him faithfully, by whose money he was bought, however illegal that traffic may be considered. In heathen countries, slavery was in some sort excusable; but among Christians it is an *enormity* and a CRIME for which perdition has scarcely an adequate state of punishment." *Dr. A. Clarke.*

Here the word rendered servants, is οἰκέται; which signifies *household servants;* but even this word does not necessarily imply those who were the entire property of another; it is true, that οἰκέτης, had this signification sometimes, among the Greeks, but not always; and the reasons before assigned, show that it is by no means probable, that this is the sense in which this word is used here. It occurs but in three other places in the New Testament, and in one of them the reader will perceive at once, that it could not have been used to signify one who was held as the entire property of another. This is Luke 16 : 13. See also, Acts 10 : 7. Rom. 14 : 4.

10. *Love as brethren.*

It is difficult to conceive what the Christian enslavers, at the south, do with this and similar passages of Scripture, as it is well known, that a minister, in many places cannot enforce the law of love without being *suspected* of favoring emancipation; and it must be remembered, that if any one in some of the states, do but make a *sign* or *utter* one *syllable*, which may be *construed* as having such a design, or a tendency to this effect, he is liable to suffer *death upon the gallows!*

12. *We ought to lay down our lives for the brethren.*

It is a strange fact, that the wicked enslavers of the human species, such as make no pretensions to any religious principle in the regulation of their conduct, will never refuse to risk their lives in their efforts to keep the slaves in bondage, and yet how few, how very few professing Christians and Christian ministers are found, who will run even the hazard of losing a little property, in order to restore to their brethren the *unalienable* RIGHTS of which they have been so unjustly deprived! If we say a word to them about doing *justice* to the poor oppressed, degraded and injured slave, we are directly told of the *consequences!* Oh the dreadful *consequences* that would follow the enactment of *just* and *suitable laws*, for the *protection, defence*, and *regulation* of the poor slaves!

Let us notice a few cases of emancipation, and see what the *consequences* were which followed. In 1820, the emperor Alexander, emancipated the whole population of the island of Oesel, amounting to no less than 35,000. No evil consequences followed. Slavery was abolished, suddenly, in 1829, by the Republic of Mexico. Columbia, another Republic of South America, did the same in 1821. Guatamala, in 1824. Peru and Chili, in 1828, and Bolivia about the same time. Buenos Ayres abolished slavery in 1816, and Monte Video more recently; many other nations who have done the same have been mentioned in another chapter. On the first of August 1834, this work was done throughout the British dominions; and in Antigua and Bermuda, where the slaves were made unconditionally free, no difficulties of any kind have followed. But in some of the other West India Islands where they undertook to obtain work from the slaves after they were *made free,* and this too without the use of the whip, or the reward of money to pay them for their labors, as was anticipated, some uneasiness has followed.

But what evil consequences could possibly follow the emancipation of all the slaves in this land, if this should be done *by the enactment of suitable and impartially administered laws?* Would the enactment of just and equitable laws for their defence and supervision, could such laws any way produce one millionth part of the wickedness which now constitutes the very sum and substance of the slave-system? Why is it that persons who talk so much about the "consequences" of abolishing slavery in this nation, never undertake to make some estimate of the world of iniquity of the system, and the ten thousand thousand evils which it is constantly bringing upon the nation, and upon all who are connected with it! Think of the *accumulated wrongs* which nearly three millions of men women and children are compelled every day and every hour, to suffer in this nation! Think of the *theft*, the *fraud*, the *pollution*, and the numberless other CRIMES which this system is now constantly inflicting, upon both the enslaver and the enslaved! And think of the death struggle which must sooner or later come between the blacks and whites at the south, if slavery be not soon abolished by moral and peaceable means.

Hear one of Virginia's statesmen, on this subject, Henry Berry, Esq., in a speech of his, delivered in the House of delegates of Va. Jan. 20. 1822.

"Sir, I believe, that no *cancer* on the physical body, was ever more *certain, steady*, and FATAL in its progress, than this cancer on the political body of Virginia. *It is eating into her very vitals.* And shall we admit, that the evil is past remedy? Shall we act the part of a puny patient, suffering under the ravages of a fatal disease, who would say the remedy is too painful? — " Pass as severe laws as you will, to keep these unfortunate creatures in ignorance, it is vain, unless you can extinguish that spark of intellect which God has given them. — Sir, *we have as far as possible* CLOSED EVERY AVENUE BY WHICH LIGHT MIGHT ENTER THEIR MINDS; we have only to go one step farther, — to extinguish the capacity to see the light, and our work will be completed; they would then be reduced to the level with the beasts of the field, and we should be safe; and I am not certain, that we would not do it, if we could find out the necessary process — and that under the plea of *necessity*. But, sir, this is impossible; and can man be in the midst of freemen and not know what freedom is? Can he feel that he has the power to assert his liberty, and will he not do it? Yes, sir, with the certainty of time's current he will do it, whenever he has the power. — The data are before us all, and every man can work out the process for himself. Sir, a *death struggle* must come between the two classes, in which one or the other will be extinguished forever. Who can contemplate such a catastrophe, as even possible, and be indifferent?"

15. *Partaker of his evil deeds.*

Let those members and ministers in the Christian church, who do not set their faces against the sin of slave-holding in all who practice it, think on these words.

16. *Slaves and souls of men.*

The σωμάτων, *bodies* and souls of men; these are here set down as articles of *traffic*, with *beasts, sheep*, and *horses!* And it should be noted also, that the trade here spoken of, in the *souls* and *bodies* of men, was carried on by an *anti-christian* church.

"The Lord who judgeth her, will effuse his wrath upon Babylon, because she makes merchandize of slaves, the souls and bodies of men. To number the persons of men with beasts, sheep, and horses, as the stock of a farm, or with bales of goods, as the cargo of a ship, is a most detestable and anti-christian practice." *Scott.*

Butf rom these words we learn, that the time is coming when NO MAN *shall buy the souls and bodies of men any more at all!* And consequently, when the souls and bodies of men are neither bought nor sold any more, then all slave-holding must cease, and slavery become extinct throughout this nation and throughout the whole world! Yes, as sure as we may depend upon the veracity of the infinite God, just so certainly we shall not be disappointed in expecting the utter extinction of this infernal system from the face of the globe. And then will come the world's JUBILEE! O the delightful anticipations of that auspicious day! When man shall enslave his fellow man " no more at all! " when there shall be " no more " soul-drivers, nor " brokers in the trade of blood." When the clanking of *chains*, upon *human limbs*, shall be heard " no more at all." When the *bloody thumb-screws* and the lacerating whip, shall torture "no more at all." Then shall the cruel man-stealer no more part those asunder whom God joins together; nor shall the parent's joy be damped and chilled any more, by the sight of the Christian white man!

Merciful God! In the greatness of thy compassion hasten, O hasten, the arrival of that blessed hour!

INDEX.

A.
Abolition, immediate, what is meant by it, Page 54
Adultery fostered by the Slave-system, 62, 63, 64
Afflicting case of a Mother, 36
America, United States of, 77
Apostles referred to, 89

B.
Blessing of him that was ready to perish, 35
Blessing pronounced upon such as remember the poor, 40
Bondage of the Israelites 14
Bond-servants, Hebrews not to be compelled to serve as such, 25
Bonds, those in, to be remembered, 93
Breaking the commands of God, and teaching men so, 73

C.
Casting lots for God's people, 70
Christian rum-drinkers, 41
Christian enslavers, 41
Clarke, Dr. A. his opinion of slavery, and the slave-trade, 55, 90, 98
Coke, Dr. his opposition to slavery, 58
Comfort of the oppressed, 48
Congress, members of, engaged in the slave-trade, 69
Consequences to be apprehended, from the continuance of the slave-system, 99
Covetousness forbidden, 27, 77
Cruelties to servants, forbidden by the Mosaic law, 22

D.
Daniel, his example referred to, 89
Definition of slavery, 9, 16
Defrauding, against, 90
Devil, the, a great oppressor, 78
Doing unto others as we would they should do unto us, 74
Dreadful sound, in the ears of oppressors, 83
Dumb, the slaves are, in a most affecting sense, 48

E.
Emancipation, immediate, a duty, 54
Emancipation, cases of, 98, 99
Example, power of, 41

F.
False-dealing forbidden, 24
False-dealing, case of stated, 24

INDEX.

G.
Gibeonites, the reasons why they were reduced to servitude, 33
Gilgrass, the Rev. Mr. his account of a mother who was robbed of her children, 36
Guilty, in what sense a person is, of breaking all of God's commandments, 96

H.
Hardening the heart, how slave-holders do this, 17
Hunting souls, 67, 68
Hypocrites, why slaves think others such, 41, 54

I.
Ignorance, no excuse for neglect of duty, in certain cases, 47
Ignorance of the slaves, how it is caused, 68, 69
Immediate emancipation, 54
Inquisition, in the United States, 39

J.
Job, his example referred to, 35
Jubilee among the Jews, 42
Jubilee of the world, predicted, 100
Judgment against such as show no mercy, 96
Justice commanded, 28

K.
Kidnappers, manner of their taking their prey, 40
Kidnapping, case of, stated, 57

L.
Laws, oppressive, 48, 89
Love commanded toward our neighbor, 25, 75, 77, 93
    toward brethren, 98
    toward our enemies, 74

M.
Mad, oppression makes men so, 49
McDowell, extract from his speech, 34
Man-stealers, 90, 91
Man-stealing, cases of stated, 57, 61
Man-thieves condemned, 28
Marshall, T. Esq., 56
Mercy, definition of this word, 72, 73
Murder may be justified in the same way that many attempt to justify slavery, 11

N.
Number oppressed in this land, 32

O.
Obedience, commanded to servants, 90
Onesimus, his case considered, 92
Oppression defined, 14
Oppressing the poor, 45, 46
Oppressing the afflicted in the gate. 46

P.

Paul, St. his chains, referred to,	90
Paxton, Rev. J. D. extracts from,	57
Pity commanded,	33
Pharaoh a slave-holder,	15
Polygamy, may be justified from the Bible, with as much propriety as slave-holding,	10
Poor, are Christ's representatives,	45
Power of masters over their slaves,	9
Preachers, slave-holding,	69
Prejudice, a sin,	45
Promises of God to deliver the oppressed,	23, 26, 40

R.

Reconciliation, to those whom we have injured, necessary before we approach God in prayer,	73
Relief, to be afforded to such as are in distress,	25
Reproaching God, how some do this,	45
Reproving our neighbor a duty,	55
Reward, not to be given, for doing justice,	55
Rich men who oppress the poor,	96

S.

Sabbatical year,	25
Scott, quotations from,	79, 91
Servant, meaning of the word so rendered in the New Testament,	93
Servitude among the Jews, &c.	22
Silence of Christ, concerning slavery,	11
Sin of oppression,	42
Slave laws of S. Carolina,	15
Slavery, what it is,	9
Souls and bodies of men, trading in,	100
Stealing forbidden,	26
Stumbling-blocks, to be removed,	24

T.

Task-masters, slave-holders in Egypt so called,	15
Theft, penalty for this crime among the Jews,	22
Trading the persons of men,	69
Traps, to catch men, described,	60, 61
Trust, in oppression,	84

W.

Wages of the laborer not to be retained,	24, 97
Waste places, caused by slavery,	56
Weightier matters of the law omitted,	76
Wesley, his testimony against slavery and the slave-trade	78, 79
Wesleyan Conference Resolutions of, against slavery,	79, 91

220.8　　　　　　　　　　83829
S958t

Sunderland
The testimony of God against slavery

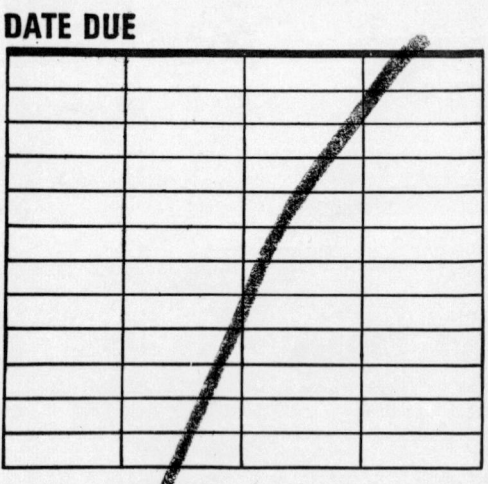

Memorial Library
Mars Hill College
Mars Hill, N. C. 28754